POOLE
PARK
THE PEOPLE'S PARK

POOLE PARK

THE PEOPLE'S PARK

GEOFFREY BUDWORTH

The History Press

First published 2008

The History Press Ltd
The Mill, Brimscombe Port
Stroud, Gloucestershire, GL5 2QG
www.thehistorypress.co.uk

British Library Cataloguing in Publication Data.
A catalogue record for this book is available from the British Library.

ISBN 978 0 7509 5092 3

Typesetting and origination by The History Press Ltd.
Printed in Great Britain

CONTENTS

INTRODUCTION

The present is the key to the past.

Sir Charles Lyell, Scottish geologist, 1797–1875

Poole Park is young as history is measured, not yet 120 years or twelve decades old, a mere one-and-a-half human life spans of eighty years laid end-to-end. Nevertheless a lot happened in that time, and others might tell its story differently, recalling other events, characters and anecdotes. This is my interpretation.

Today the Borough of Poole is a Conservative-controlled unitary authority, whose elected councillors and salaried officers model and mould a town and its surrounding area with a population of 141,000 (but rising fast), managing the demands of business, tourism and leisure, plus more than sixty open spaces, including the historic Upton House with the 100-acre Upton Country Park and, of course, Poole Park.

Prominent employers include Barclays Bank, Penske Cars (the successful Indy racing team), and Ryvita.

Poole Pottery (established in 1873) is currently rebuilding with a state-of-the-art studio and visitor centre; the Lighthouse Arts Centre is the largest outside London; and the greyhound stadium is also the base for the Poole Pirates speedway team.

Poole is home to Bournemouth University, the Arts Institute of Bournemouth, and the Bournemouth Symphony Orchestra. Then again, since the introduction in 2004 of citizenship ceremonies, over 400 have been conducted in Poole for applicants relocating from Iran, Iraq, Pakistan, South Africa, Turkey, America and Zimbabwe.

Poole's natural harbour, the largest in Europe, lies atop a commercial oil field. The harbour commissioners regulate the disparate activities of the RNLI headquarters and training school, the Special Boat Section (SBS) of the Royal Marines, and Sunseeker International, who build the most stylish and luxurious motor yachts; while from a busy terminal, Condor and Brittany ferries daily convey commercial and private vehicles, their drivers and passengers, to and from the Channel Islands and France. The largest of its five islands, Brownsea Island – the site of the first Boy Scout camp in 1907 – is now owned by the National Trust, with the south east leased to the John Lewis Partnership for staff holidays. The harbour has boatyards and marinas, plus Rockley Watersports (the south coast's premier sailing school), and it hosts the UK's supreme wind and kite surfing championships.

Poole's beaches have held the coveted Blue Flag accreditation for the last twenty years, and the Sandbanks peninsula – one of the most expensive residential areas in the world, with its multi-million pound waterside mansions – has been dubbed the St Tropez of the south coast.

Despite, or perhaps because of, the town's pedigree of piracy and smuggling, Queen Elizabeth I in 1568 granted by Great Charter to Poole the unique status of being both a town *and* a county, distinct and separate from the county of Dorset. So it became 'the Borough and County of the Town of Poole'. This effectively ended any control over it by the lord of

Albert Cottages, home of the park's first gardeners. (Author's collection)

the manor. The dual status lapsed with the local government reorganisation of 1974, but was restored to the town when it became a unitary authority in 1997. The following year Poole celebrated its 750th birthday.

The charter allows the town to elect not only its own mayor but also a sheriff, now one of only fifteen including London with that privilege; although today the sheriff's role is diminished to an honorary one, supporting the mayor and deputy mayor in their civic duties and responsibilities – and they boast the longest-serving town crier (fifty years) in England.

The town's fishermen once enjoyed exclusive fishing rights, awarded them by Queen Victoria, off Labrador and Newfoundland (indeed, some say that the unusual 'Newfie' accent may be partly due to a flavour of Dorset dialect). And into the twentieth century imported timber was unloaded at the quayside, as well as coal on an industrial scale destined for the local gas works, and for domestic use locally (and in the fast-growing smart seaside resort of Bournemouth a few miles to the east).

The old town of Poole has been extensively demolished and so rebuilt that it is now almost unrecognisable from the scene in 1890 when 7,800 residents existed in multi-occupied, low-rent housing that was overcrowded and poorly maintained by neglectful landlords. Although the quayside remained active with as many as 1,000 ships a year, bringing 180,000 tons of goods in and out of the port, the loss of the lucrative trans-Atlantic trade and fishing links resulted in mass unemployment. The wealthy moved out, leaving behind the working class and jobless, reducing the town – some observed – to almshouses, narrow alleyways and slum tenements, dereliction, demolition and drunks. Judges and justices were kept busy in crowded courtrooms as Poole was frequently required to assist the police with their enquiries.

Britain as a whole, with its strong economy and powerful navy, nevertheless remained the most influential nation in the world. The British Empire covered roughly one quarter of the planet's land mass, on which it was said 'the sun never set', and ruled one quarter of its population. Queen Victoria, celebrating her Golden Jubilee in 1887, reigned over what was perceived to be a golden age of peace (ignoring far-off colonial conflicts). The lawful school leaving age was ten years and home rule for Ireland was an unresolved issue, but Prime Minister William Ewart Gladstone, a Liberal reformer, would be re-elected to serve a fourth consecutive term of office and elected Jews and atheists were permitted to take their seats in the House of Commons.

Above and below: Early vistas of the park. (Author's collection)

Inventions during this era included the pneumatic tyre, alloy steel, the seismograph, and – in a chilling hint of the coming First World War, still a generation in the future – the production of cordite and the first fully-automatic Maxim machine gun.

Gilbert & Sullivan's opera *The Gondoliers* was in the middle of its three-year run at the Savoy Theatre in London; Thomas Hardy was writing *Tess of the D'Urbervilles*; Oscar Wilde had scandalised readers with *The Picture of Dorian Gray* (first published that year in *Lippincott's Magazine*); while Robert Louis Balfour Stevenson, Henry Rider Haggard and Arthur Conan Doyle were all consolidating their considerable reputations.

This was the age when the Corporation of the Borough of Poole created its park for the people.

Pre-Victorian fun and games went on in streets and fields, on common land, or at fairgrounds. Then, in the late nineteenth century, public-health initiatives led to the first public parks complemented by aviaries and fountains, bandstands and boating lakes.

The notion of a people's park had been debated by Poole Council on and off for twenty years before, in the early 1880s, they bought a plot of land from Lord Wimborne, for £100 an acre, covering twenty acres (eight hectares) between Kingland Road and the area used by Longfleet Ropeworks known as Ladies Walking Field. This was intended to become both a park and a recreation ground, but, when the borough surveyor John Elford tried to draw up plans, he discovered that the site was unsuitable for either purpose (although an open-air swimming pool was built).

Lord Wimborne – Sir Ivor Bertie Guest – had become the Lord of Canford Magna at the age of twenty-one in August 1856, his father having died four years earlier; but it was not until after his marriage in 1868 to Lady Cornelia Churchill that he took over his responsibilities as lord of the manor and made Canford House, a little to the south-west of Wimborne and six miles north of Poole, his home. The Manor of Canford was recorded in the Domesday Book of 1086 (although there would be no mention of the fishing port of Poole until early in the thirteenth century) and his lordship's extensive estate comprised some 16,000 acres.

He was made Baron Wimborne of Canford Magna in 1880 by his friend Lord Beaconsfield at the end of that statesman's last term of office as Prime Minister, and proved to be a generous man as well as a considerate landlord. But it was his wife, Lady Cornelia, the eldest daughter of John Churchill, 7th Duke of Marlborough, who seems to have been the driving force. She was an eloquent speaker and a fast talker who, according to Mr P.E.L. Budge, the solicitor-agent of the Conservatives in Poole (and its mayor on two occasions) '… had an irresistible means of getting her own way …' Certainly she is credited for the gift of land that would form Poole Park and for which she and Lord Wimborne are now best remembered.

In May 1885 an embarrassed corporation approached Lord Wimborne again, this time with a view to purchasing land north of Parkstone Bay, and they were relieved and delighted when (without referring to their previous agreement) his lordship wrote to the mayor, Mr William Mate and offered to give the Borough, free of charge, fifteen parcels of land amounting to thirty-three acres, two roods and twenty-nine perches (about thirteen hectares) comprising garden allotments, arable land, pasture, meadow and marsh.

Forty years ago, Poole Park consisted of a small farm on the higher ground and a few marshy meadows over which a precarious footpath wound its devious way … the waterlogged part has been drained and the water collected into pretty little lakes with willowy islands where there are stately swans and quaint Egyptian geese and other waterfowl … the marsh where the present writer in his youth sought for water plants while the snipe hummed around and the haunting cry of the lapwing pursued the course of the intruder is now a splendid cricket ground, so good that the great county cricket matches are played there.

Extract from the *Town Guide*, 1910

This area had been part of the tidal Poole harbour's shallow backwaters until eleven years earlier, in 1875, when the London & South Western Railway Co. had isolated it by building a causeway and single train track. It was soggy, with brackish drainage channels that would have to be filled in and levelled, but the location was ideal, and his lordship's only condition was that the land must be 'laid out and planted … as a public park and pleasure ground for the Borough of Poole and the inhabitants thereof and others who may use the same … for ever'. The council promptly accepted this generous gift, which was confirmed on an imperial-sized document measuring 27in by 22in, dated 3 March 1896, in legalistic manuscript, together with a hand-tinted plan of the land and lake and authenticated with a 10s. stamp (240 times the value of the ½d. postage stamp then needed to send a postcard by the Royal Mail).

In mid-1886 a national competition was held to design the park and the winner was the Exeter landscaping firm of Veitch & Son, (although their design later proved too costly to implement), while E. W. Upsil of Wandsworth, London, was runner-up. They were duly awarded prizes of £25 and £10 respectively.

Then a legal setback emerged. The council was keen to acquire an extra part of the Parkstone Bay foreshore enclosed by the railway that was not included in Lord Wimborne's gift. He demurred but said that he would let the corporation have it on a ninety-nine-year-lease for 1s. a year. In fact it was doubtful whether it was his to give or sell, as the Crown Commissioners had long asserted that the foreshore belonged to the Crown. A few years earlier however, in 1885, Parliament had modified the relevant statute to allow gifts to corporations to become legal on the anniversary of the gift so long as the donor was still alive. This meant a twelve-month delay. It was irksome but gave the borough surveyor John Elford time to persuade the council that yet more land was needed for a satisfactory park layout; and so, during the intervening months, they bought a total of fifteen extra acres, some 'at the back of Mr Saunders house' and some from Lord Wimborne.

The delay also gave the council breathing space to negotiate with the railway company, then busy doubling its tracks atop the embankment, to construct an archway giving access to the proposed park from the east and south of the borough, high enough to provide for the passage of a carriage (even if its base was below sea level). This is the keyhole bridge … which still floods during heavy rain. It also gave the council time to settle the details with the railway for a sluice to be provided through the embankment to control the water level in the lake.

Fresh plans for the park by John Elford and his newly appointed Dutch surveyor Edmund Van Schepdael were approved and the contract given to Messrs Veitch & Son, whose efforts would result in one of the most picturesque pleasure grounds to be found anywhere in England, enclosed by smart iron railings and gates on impressive brick-built pillars ornamented with terracotta sea-life dressings, topped by eagles and globe lamps. The two main gates were guarded by lodges. A layout of roads and pathways linked attractions within the park that included a cricket ground, a cycle track and tennis lawns. By means of the sluice gates in the railway embankment, the massive saltwater lake could be kept at a safe depth for boating, while a smaller freshwater lake and a duck pond were havens for swans, ducks and other water fowl. The total estimated cost was £7,630.

Edwardian youngsters utilize the boating lake in 1904. (Author's collection)

The freshwater lake seen on a winter's evening. (Geoffrey Budworth)

THE NOT-SO-GRAND OPENING

Everything that can possibly go wrong will go wrong.
Attributed to USAF aerospace pioneers George E. Nichols, Edward Murphy
and John Paul Stapp, *c.* 1952

In 1889 the Mayor of Poole received a letter from Lord Wimborne informing him that, the following January, Edward Prince of Wales was to visit Canford Manor with Princess Alexandra and their children. His lordship felt sure that, if formally asked to do so by the corporation, His Royal Highness would be pleased to open both Poole and Parkstone Parks. So the Prince's consent was sought and given.

Sheriff Christopher Hill called a public meeting to form a committee to organise the event and raise funds. The mayor began the collection with a donation of £30. The date was fixed for Saturday 18 January 1890, when the royal party would drive from Parkstone, where HRH would first open the much smaller inland public park there, to a large marquee pavilion erected in Poole Park where the grand (ticket holders only) ceremonial opening would be performed. From there the royal visitors would go in procession through the streets of Old Poole to the railway station and board their train at 1.30 p.m. for the return to London.

As it happened, however, the Princess and her two daughters, Victoria and Maud, remained at Marlborough House, disabled with severe colds which it was feared might be the Siberian 'flu epidemic, then widespread. In Canford Manor, Lord Wimborne too had gone to bed with feverish aches and pains.

When the Prince arrived at Wimborne railway station on Wednesday 15 January, he was accompanied by his sons Prince Albert Victor and Prince Albert George, with Prince Hohenlohe, the Governor of Alsace Lorraine. So the royal train brought two potential monarchs – the future King Edward VII and his successor George V. They were met with a carriage and four by Ivor and Montagu Guest, two of Lord Wimborne's sons and, as they exited the tastefully decorated and illuminated station, a 100-strong crowd of local people cheered their arrival. They were also saluted by a detachment of the Dorset (Queen's Own) Yeomanry and the Wimborne Volunteers.

Their immediate destination was Canford Manor, a Victorian mansion without equal in Dorset. Little of the original medieval building then remained, except the kitchen, as its previous owner had rebuilt in mock-Gothic style to feature a courtyard, a gigantic entrance tower (rated by Nikolaus Pevsner as one of Charles Barry's best), a great hall, a monumental staircase, a conservatory, a library and an exhibition room. Despite a major fire six years earlier, in 1884, which had destroyed the main staircase and ruined many fine tapestries, paintings and china, the house had been restored and a new wing added in 1887.

During Lady Cornelia's tenure there was a constant procession of royal guests and ruling statesmen, as well as frequent Conservative fêtes, horticultural shows, tennis tournaments, cricket matches and shooting parties. At one Primrose League gathering in 1885 it was reported that over 30,000 attended despite torrential rain. So it was nothing remarkable that on this occasion many friends of the Prince and Lady Cornelia had been invited as house guests, including a marquis and marchioness, an earl, a viscount and viscountess (or two), peers of the realm, lords and ladies. All had been done to make their stay enjoyable, from outdoor shooting to indoor billiards.

The Prince however had little time for such diversions; the day after his arrival was devoted to a full programme of engagements in drizzling rain at Bournemouth. These were attended by the Mayor of Poole Mr Philip E. Lionel Budge who, with his two sergeants-at-mace (all in flamboyant new robes purchased for the occasion), made quite an impact themselves upon the onlookers; and his worship no doubt felt confident that the Corporation of Poole would, in its turn, make a good impression in two-days' time.

The streets from Parkstone Park to Poole Park, as well as those of Old Poole, had been lavishly decorated, with splendid triumphal arches constructed in Lower Parkstone and Poole High Street. In front of the large marquee pavilion was an imposing, life-size model of the old town wall and gates of Poole, through which the Prince and his entourage were to drive. A band had been hired to play in the pavilion. If planning could make it so, it would be a memorable royal visit.

The Prince had no formal commitments the following day, other than Lady Cornelia's evening reception at Canford House, to which all the local dignitaries as well as the commanding officers of the Army and Navy detachments involved in the following day's proceedings had been invited. A grand ball had been planned but, since Augusta, Empress of Germany had died the week before, decorum required the ladies of Dorset to discard their festive gowns for dresses of subdued hues, and the dancing was cancelled. Still, electricity had been installed, with thousands of lamps, so that the otherwise sombre occasion was nevertheless a dazzling scene.

But outdoors was ominous. The weather had been dreary for a fortnight and at 3 a.m. on Saturday, as the mayor and his companions left to climb into their carriages, they were hit by hurricane-force wind and blinding rain. The severe storm only abated at daybreak to reveal ruined decorations and a wrecked pavilion.

The mayor, after an urgent exchange of telegrams with Canford House, decided to delay proceedings while work went ahead to salvage at least some of the street decorations. Prince Edward would tour Poole town, as promised, before declaring Poole Park open in a ceremony to be arranged on the platform of the railway station prior to boarding his train. It would be a disappointing second best.

At 11 a.m. members of the council and magistrates assembled at the Guildhall. Aldermen and councillors all wore new gowns, the sheriff had a cocked hat, and the town clerk wore his wig, for an informal procession to be escorted by two members of the borough police on horseback and a dozen members of the Bristol mounted police.

At 12.30 p.m., the Dorset Yeomanry Hussars, in dress uniform and with drawn swords, set off from Canford House at the head of a royal cortège of carriages led by the Prince of Wales, Lady Cornelia Wimborne, Prince George and Prince Hohenlohe, followed by other house guests. When the Prince's carriage drew up before the assembled members of the council, the mayor formally welcomed him to the borough, before taking his place in a grand carriage, with mounted postilions provided by him. His two sergeants-at-mace climbed into the box seats and he then led the procession on its journey through the town. Local policemen, augmented by eight officers from the Dorset Constabulary, fifty from Hampshire and twenty from far-off Southampton took up positions on those roads closed for the procession, and in places schoolchildren lined the route.

As the column moved off, scores of conveyances of all kinds, from horse-drawn four-wheeled phaetons to humble dog carts fell in behind; some youngsters chased shouting after the carriages and others ran through shortcuts to intercept the column at intervals. It was, witnesses later recalled, not so much a state drive as like following a foxhunt. Nevertheless, the sun shone brightly for the first time in weeks, and the welcome given the Prince by 'a motley crowd of farmers, peasants and sailors' after their long wait was a friendly, if boisterous, one.

Some street decorations had survived the storm. Others had been retrieved and restored. The most elaborate of four triumphal arches was an enormous replica of Poole's old town wall, 100ft wide, with a 33ft-high three-storey tower and battlements topped by a flagstaff flying the Royal Standard. Two mock-stone gateways across the two carriageways of the new park had imitation ramparts which bore the painted inscription 'Welcome to our Ancient Borough' on one side, with 'Welcome to the Prince of Wales' and 'The Nation's Pride' on the other. Having passed through these the original plan had, of course, been for the Prince and honoured guests to be greeted by the mayor outside the pavilion and led to seats of honour in the great marquee, where the Bournemouth Silver Band would strike up the National Anthem. But the once majestic pavilion was a collapsed mass of sodden canvas, writhing in the wind, upon the wrecked staging and seating.

The procession continued through streets of houses flying flags and bunting to the quayside, where the Poole lifeboat was on display with its crew standing at attention alongside it in souwesters and cork lifebelts. The fire brigade lined up, immaculate in their uniforms, with gleaming engines, fire escapes and equipment. The crews of ships berthed at the quayside manned yardarms, in both a demonstration of seamanship and to gain a better view. Church bells pealed. A choir of orphan girls sang *God Bless the Prince of Wales*. The Volunteer Artillery Band played the National Anthem. It was, despite setbacks, a right royal welcome.

But a further trial awaited the mayor. The railway police had not been consulted about the change of plan and, when the mayor arrived at the station only minutes ahead of the Prince, they expressed concern for His Royal Highness's safety on an exposed platform. If the opening ceremony for Poole Park was to take place on railway property, they insisted, it must do so indoors.

There was no time to argue. The mayor turned to welcome the Prince as he arrived at the booking office with Lady Cornelia and the young Princes, apologising for yet another improvisation. He then presented the sheriff and town clerk and asked the Prince to receive an illuminated address of loyalty from the town. This the Prince of Wales did and, as it was pointless to read their prepared speeches to one other in the privacy of the little booking office, he simply handed the mayor the text of his intended speech on opening the park (in which, it was later found, he expressed himself 'deeply interested in the important question of providing open-air spaces for the inhabitants of towns' and saying that it gave him 'the greatest satisfaction in opening the park and recreation ground'). Lady Cornelia presented the Prince with a bouquet of orchids which she asked him to give to the sick Princess of Wales.

Outside on the station platform, members of the council, the magistrates and other notable guests had been carefully arranged to greet and meet the royal party … but all they saw was the Prince and his entourage saying their goodbyes as they boarded the train. The Handel String Band, hastily recruited to play, were taken utterly by surprise when they were suddenly called upon to perform and struck up in tuneless confusion.

So, at 1.30 p.m., the Prince of Wales gave the assembly a farewell smile, there was much hat raising, and the train moved off (but in the unexpected direction of Weymouth). A few minutes later, having cleared the points, it reappeared on the London-bound up-line, the Prince of Wales standing at the saloon window and bowing in response to the passing cheers. He would reach London at 4 p.m.

By 2 p.m. those left behind in Poole were at a corporation luncheon in honour of Lady Cornelia in the newly decorated Guildhall. For it was to her that Mayor Budge gave most of the credit for Poole having achieved its park. He also praised those officers of the corporation, especially John Elford and Edmund van Schepdael, who designed the amenity. His Royal Highness, he reported, had expressed his pleasure with the reception and the arrangements, thinking the park and everything connected with the place looked very good, and that the town was certainly beautifully decorated for the occasion.

Buoyed up (or at least with little time to be downcast), having survived the morning, the mayor later hosted a tea in the Amity Hall for 700 people over sixty years of age, with entertainment that included a conjuror from Southampton. But the blustery weather returned and illuminations planned for the evening were abandoned. So the mayor's last engagement that day was his visit to inmates of the workhouse.

Lord Wimborne died in 1914 at the age of seventy-nine. Ivor Churchill Guest, already a peer in his own right as Baron Ashby St Leger (and, at the time of his father's death, Lord-in-Waiting to George V) succeeded his father. The following year he was appointed Lord Lieutenant of Ireland, a post he retained until the end of the war in 1918, when he was created Viscount Wimborne.

The new lord of the manor evinced no interest in Canford or the affairs of Poole, although he did nothing to disturb his family until after Lady Cornelia's death in 1927, when he put up for sale those parts of the estate that were financially unproductive (such as the golf courses). A few years later a buyer was found for Canford House itself which, with its park, is now a co-education public boarding school.

Soon all respect and regard for their lord and his lady at Canford House by the people of Poole turned to suspicion and distrust of its latest incumbent. The British author and poet Hilaire Belloc, a Liberal MP, wrote bitterly of him:

> Grant, O Lord, eternal rest
> To they servant, Ivor Guest,
> Never mind the where or how,
> Only grant it to him now.

Poole remains indebted, however, to Lord Wimborne and Lady Cornelia for their many acts of generosity more than 100 years ago, and, despite its chaotic opening, Poole Park is their enduring memorial.

AROUND & ABOUT THE PARK: AN A–Z GLOSSARY

It's as large as life, and twice as natural.

Lewis Carroll, English author, 1832–1898

This glossary augments the Guided Walk, with extra facts and figures, so together they make a more fact-packed account of the park.

AVIARY

Caged birds accept each other but flight is what they long for.

Tennessee Williams, American playwright, 1911–1983

Just prior to the First World War a bird enclosure was opened in an area of grass and trees close to the cycle track. Some of the first occupants were five peacocks (two male, three female); but, after complaints about their strident calls, these birds were removed to Brownsea Island, where they bred, and now there are more than 200. Captive birds do not seem to incense animal-welfare activists in the same way as caged animals, but, as the aviary became part of Poole Park's zoo in 1963, it too disappeared when the zoo was shut down and demolished in 1994 (see Zoo).

BOATING

There is nothing – absolutely nothing – half so much worth doing as simply messing about in boats.

Kenneth Graham, Scottish author, 1859–1932

With an average depth of 4ft (1.2m), the saltwater lake in Poole Park was always going to be used as a summer boating lagoon – but not, in the early 1900s, on Sundays.

The first hire boats were built by Arthur Vincent Shutler who owned and operated his fleet of heavy clinker-built rowing skiffs, canoes, kayaks, sailing dinghies and stable double-ended craft (for children) – propelled by a pair of hand-turned paddle wheels – from around 1900 onwards. Some of the boats had names – *The Favourite* and *Hetty Davis* were just two recalled by older residents but some later craft were known by letters of the Greek alphabet (Alpha, Beta, Gamma etc.) and others simply had numbers painted on their bows.

The next boat master was a Mr Baker, who was followed in about 1947 by Peter Pulsford. He paid a flat-rate rent of £300 a year to the council for the boating franchise, although later owner/operators would be charged a percentage of their takings.

Above and below: Aviary, birds and bystanders. (Andrew Hawkes)

Arthur Vincent Shutler (nearest the camera) with his hire-boat crew. (Andrew Hawkes)

A blustery day for boating in 1930. (Andrew Hawkes)

In the 1930s an area of the lake was boomed off into two small lagoons, one to contain silent battery-driven electric 'glider' boats, the other to be occupied by small petrol-driven motorboats.

George Vimpany (see Miniature Railway) bought out Peter Pulsford and took on the boat hire lease around 1957, and in 1975 he sold the business to Geoff Tapper who, as a schoolboy helped out Peter Pulsford unpaid, before going on to employed by him in 1953. Geoff added to the hard-worked and ageing fleet of around seventy-five wooden craft, buying or building extra craft, and introducing fibreglass construction to the traditional larch and other wooden hulls. He once bought a boat in Swanage which he and a friend then rowed around by sea, entering Poole harbour to land at Whitecliff, then portaging via the keyhole bridge. They relaunched in the lake and completed the final few 100yds of their 10-mile odyssey to the boathouse located on the promontory where now stands the Mezza Luna Restaurant (see Catering)

Photographs from the 1980s show adults and children operating radio-controlled (token-operated) motor boats on a mini marina in front of the small car park to the east of the war memorial.

QUEEN OF THE LAKE

In 1984 Geoff introduced a 22ft-long replica of a Mississippi-style stern-wheel paddle boat. Having planned to build one himself, he first spotted this ready-made version at a Butlin's holiday camp, later tracked it down to a Milton Keynes fairground, and finally bought it from a marine yard. It was in a dilapidated condition but he restored and licensed it for use in the park.

The *Queen of the Lake* was ceremonially launched on the lake in July by the Mayoress of Poole, Mrs Mollie Breckell, for whom the bottle of champagne failed to shatter until Geoff lent a hand. The largest craft regularly on the lake, it seated twenty passengers and was adapted for wheelchair users. Although the twin paddle wheels did not propel the boat – that was done by outboard engines – they turned with the movement of the boat through the water. Tricked out with fretwork and pointy bits, the illusion completed by make-belief twin funnels braced with struts and stays, she was used to ferry passengers from point to point across and around the lake rather than only as a floating bit of fun and so was exempt or zero-rated for VAT.

In 1988 the *Queen of the Lake* began her fourth season afloat on the lake, freshly painted in blue and red, with a new outboard motor and added bow thrusters to assist manoeuvrability when coming alongside. The following year Scotland's strongest man came to Geoff Tapper's aid when the *Queen of the Lake* had to be lifted from the water for her winter overhaul. Sixty-two-year-old John Gallacher of Lower Parkstone, who had held the World Masters' Power Lifting title, took the strain of almost a ¼ton when he lifted a corner of the vessel to help ease it out of the lake and onto a winch system. For John, recovering from a hamstring injury and preparing for a return to international competition, it was a useful training session.

Back in August 1983 the council had voiced its concern that the boats were dilapidated and their boatmen scruffy. Geoff Tapper conceded that he had little or spare cash to reinvest in the business as takings were down, but pointed out that it was dirty work manhandling, cleaning and repairing boats that were used, misused and abused by hirers who could be over enthusiastic or downright clumsy and careless.

By 1992 a council committee was once more complaining that the image of the ageing fleet of boats, its boatyard and staff was unacceptable. Elected members and their officers were determined to include the boating concession in the recently adopted value-for-money process of compulsory competitive tendering. Meantime they proposed that Geoff Tapper should be granted an interim one-year licence instead if his usual seven-year renewal term.

A very public dispute ensued. Geoff asserted the proposal could ruin him. Did they want to put him out of business? No, replied the council. Indeed, they hoped that, as a local man, he would keep the concession and, belatedly, they agreed to a reduced rent that should release cash to replace some of the boats. He would still be given a one-year licence, however, and required to submit a formal presentation and business plan, with the chance to negotiate a seven-year lease before other operators were invited to an auction.

Geoff had run the boat hire concession on the lake for twenty years but, with the fleet lying idle due to the appearance of toxic algae, (see Saltwater Lake) he had earned nothing of his anticipated summer takings from Easter to the end of September 1995. Struggling to pay ten seasonal workers and a self-employed boat repairer, he demanded compensation and threatened the council with legal action.

From 1995–1998 the saltwater lake was plagued with toxic algae, at its worst during each summer holiday season, so that boating had to be suspended. So, despite taking on a new partner in 1997, John Withers, an ex-*Daily Echo* sailing correspondent, to manage the newly named Poole Park Boat Hire, Geoff Tapper continued to lose money but received no compensation.

From enjoying a thriving business in 1975, with over 100 boats, he had been reduced by 2002 to running at a considerable loss with just twenty-five craft. Then at the age of fifty-nine, he was given notice to quit by Poole Council and reluctantly began the process of removing every remaining boat and piece of equipment.

POWERBOATS

When Europe's only Powerboat & Watersports Show came to Poole Arts Centre on Saturday and Sunday 5 and 6 February 1994, the council gave their go-ahead for S850cc and the more powerful Formula 1 craft to stage mock races on the lake between 1–2 p.m. on Saturday, and again between 11.30–2.30 p.m. on Sunday. As expected, some local residents opposed the decision, fearing the impact of noise, pollution, and that the event might be just the first of many to alter the park from a tranquil retreat into an arena for fairground fun. Further concerns were for the well being of the waterfowl and because the event would mean putting off the annual draining that controlled water quality and minimised the amount of midges.

The council too had second thoughts when, during demonstration racing on the preceding Monday in Poole harbour, an S850cc (Formula 4) boat hit a wave, veered off course, and sliced across the stationary rigid inflatable boat from which *Bournemouth Evening Echo* photographer Helen Freeman was snapping pictures. She was seriously injured and needed an operation to repair a tendon in her leg. Shocked powerboat driver Paul Harris also received treatment.

After consulting with the sport's governing bodies and the show organisers, a split decision by councillors allowed the demonstration of racing to go ahead, and a sizeable crowd lined the lakeside to see three classes of powerboat in action. The smallest were the tiny hydroplanes, fitted with 400cc engines, in which the drivers lay prone. In almost ideal calm conditions a trio of these competed in three friendly races and the sound levels were well within the prescribed limits. The S850cc Formula 4 boats included two female drivers, one of them the veteran sixty-year-old champion Erika Erla.

Most spectacular were the two 70hp Formula 1 boats, making their first appearance on the south coast, which in full race trim were capable of speeds of up to 200km/h (over 120mph). Limited to tight circuits of the lake, and in shallow water (a safe depth of at least 6ft of water is mandatory before risking a capsize) drivers Les Liddiard and Andy Elliott still achieved 160km/h (100mph).

A balmy day in the 1970s. (Geoff Tapper)

The boating lake in 1988 with Poole Harbour and Sandbanks peninsula beyond. (Michael J. Allen Photography)

Queen of the Lake approaching the model motorboat enclosure. (Michael J. Allen Photography)

Queen of the Lake with Geoff Tapper at the wheel. (Geoff Tapper)

A disconsolate Geoff Tapper in 2002 with his redundant boats. (*Bournemouth Daily Echo*)

ROCKLEY WATERSPORTS

After a brief but unsuccessful attempt at the park's boat-hire business by a Parkstone company in the early 2000s, the lake was again bereft of boats. Until in 2007 Peter and Lis Gordon, directors of Rockley Watersports, the south of England's premier sailing school submitted the winning bid. Qualified and RYA-approved instructors offered a selection of taster sessions and structured short courses, as well as holiday camps for eight to fifteen-year-olds, with activities that include sailing, kayaking, windsurfing and orienteering. Their colourful range of at least fifty brand-new rowing boats, canoes or kayaks, sailing dinghies and windsurfers resuscitated the moribund waterside. Adrian Forte (see Catering) offered convenient storage within the Mezza Luna Restaurant, standing on the site of the demolished old boat house, which the Gordons converted into male and female changing cubicles, toilet facilities and hanging space for wet suits and buoyancy aids.

This speculative venture is meeting its business-plan forecasts despite a first year of prolonged periods of dreary weather, and promises to become a viable enterprise as predicted. Particularly reassuring has been the keenness of local schools to adopt the boating laid on by Rockley Watersports as extra-curricula group activities. The seven pedalos have proved surprisingly popular with those who simply turn up to pay and play and two dragon boats, each capable of being crewed by twenty-two paddlers, (plus a drummer to keep time) cater for those who indulge in corporate team building and sponsored events. The company even offers gift vouchers. Where prices are too much for anyone on a low incomes or disabled, or in full-time education, then the Borough of Poole's Access to Leisure and Learning discount scheme may assist in reducing the usual cost.

The polypropylene and polyester craft of Rockley Watersports in 2007. (Author's collection)

More fun than an exercise bike; the park's latest black swan. (Geoffrey Budworth)

Poole Park

The Edwardian tea house, with customers seated *al fresco* close by the cricket pitch. (Author's collection)

CATERING

One cannot think well, love well, sleep well, unless one has dined well.
Virginia Woolf, English novelist, critic and essayist, 1882–1941

The original pre-Second World War refreshment house was a red-brick building with a tiled roof and an entrance portico supported by black-painted timbers, where lunch could be enjoyed for 2s. Alternatively, seated at one of the tables outside, beneath the shade of several trees, it was possible to consume tea and cake while watching either a cricket match or the wildfowl. This establishment was run by the Forte family who originated from an Italian village between Rome and Naples.

In 1960 the council obtained central government approval to borrow £32,000 and replace the old tearooms with a new café. Work was delayed five months by a shortage of steel before it was completed and let to Anthony Forte (a second-generation son of the Forte family) who named it Swan Lake. One-third of the building would operate as a lavishly furnished grill room, the rest was a cafeteria, the two sections separated by a partition which could be drawn back to combine them for large functions. The first of these was an opening-night dance organised in December 1961 by the Poole & District branch of the National and Local Government Officers' Association (NALGO), when the borough magistrates granted an occasional liquor licence until midnight but stated it was not to be regarded as a precedent. This licence extended the sale and consumption of intoxicating liquor later than the usual permitted hours on condition that it was 'ancillary' (as the Licensing Act called it) to the service of substantial meals; in other words, beer or wine with dinner was allowed, but a round of drinks with simple snacks would be an offence.

So, on the evening in question, proceedings were observed through the curtains by a police inspector, and this officer noted that alcoholic drinks had been bought and drunk for an hour and a half before, and again after, the service of the meal. Local government officers could evidently be convivial. While no prosecution ensued, details of this police surveillance were given to magistrates when applied to later by the Swan Lake's licensee for another occasional licence to serve drinks until 11.45 p.m. at a company dinner dance. The bench accepted Chief Superintendent Jack Gray's contention that the sale and consumption of alcoholic liquor on the previous occasion had not been ancillary to the meal and, after hearing that the dinner subject to the application then under consideration would be served between 7.30–8.30 p.m., granted a parsimonious extension from 7.15–8.45 p.m.

The old tearooms had been exempted from paying business rates, the corporation having argued successfully that it was an amenity for people using the park with any profit offset against the expenses of its provision. On the assumption that the Swan Lake would be similarly free from rates, and to try to calm the political arguments in the council about the policy of the café being operated by private enterprise, a high rental was negotiated. Unfortunately, as the grill room had been widely advertised as a restaurant to which patrons were invited whether or not as park visitors, and it was to be open in the evening when most of the parks' other amenities had closed for the day, eating there could no longer be deemed as a part of park usage. So the Swan Lake became subject to rates.

With the extra burden of paying rates, the grill room proved unprofitable, and in 1966 Anthony Forte asked the corporation for a revision of his lease. The committee refused and the competing company Banquets of Oxford Ltd, already the lessee of Poole's beach cafés and kiosks at the time, took over the Swan Lake. In 1968, they were able to negotiate a revision of the terms whereby the whole café, including the grill room, could be made available for evening functions, but daytime usage of the grill room would be maintained for twelve months from June 1968. After receiving the financial results for the grill room over that period, the council reluctantly agreed that it should be discontinued and the area included in the café.

In the early 1990s Adrian Forte (a director of South Coast Catering), son of Anthony, and grandson of the family's original caterer in the park, took on the lease of the Swan Lake Café (renamed the Cygnet Café). In 1999, he spent £150,000 refurbishing the forty-year-old establishment, obtained a license for the sale of alcoholic drinks and employed eight full-time staff and fifteen part-timers. In recognition of his enterprise, and the hope that his investment would help to kick-start their planned regeneration of the park, the Corporation granted him a twenty-year lease on the premises.

MEZZA LUNA RESTAURANT

When the council, hoping to enliven evenings within the park, invited tenders for a new waterside restaurant, Adrian Forte submitted the winning bid. Apart from the Cygnet Café, his other local commitments included the Vesuvio Restaurant overlooking the beach and sea at Alum Chine, as well as a French-style café in central Bournemouth, establishing a dependable reputation.

The installation of a contemporary building within a heritage park was a radical policy decision needing nice judgement. Council officers had to overcome concern expressed by the Environment Agency about it being within their designated flood plain, as well as the collective petition of fifty-six names and thirty-two individual letters of objection from local residents fearing noise and disturbance from a 'caviar and champagne' venue.

The stylish two-tiered structure, built by the Dorset-based firm of Oates Construction to a design by Adrian and his Iraqi business partner Fidel Jobir, was curved into a crescent shape so

Above and below: The Mezza Luna Restauraunt, opened in 2007. (Geoffrey Budworth)

The Mezza Luna's curved footprint preserves mature evergreen oak trees. (Geoffrey Budworth)

as to preserve and accommodate a couple of mature evergreen holm oak (*Quercus ilex*) trees, aptly native to the Mediterranean region. The development also incorporated an outlet for takeaway food and for real Italian ice cream.

Opened on schedule in June 2007, the Mezza Luna Restaurant (Latin for half moon) caters during the day for customers buying snacks and meals, who may eat and drink indoors or sit out and view the boating activities but, in the evenings it operates as a more formal restaurant with an upstairs bar and is within an easy walk for theatre-goers from the Lighthouse Arts Centre. Chef Francesco, from southern Italy, makes a feature of Italian ingredients including seafood.

The Mezza Luna was, however, only part of a £1.7m investment by Adrian Forte in the park, taking into account a revamp of the Cygnet Café (now renamed Central Park), part of which became a 35ft by 30ft indoor skating rink of real ice, with helpful skate marshals, instructors, and special après-skating party-meal deals. This conversion squeezed the café into a long and narrow diner with mostly banquette seating and a limited menu. Families who recall Sunday lunches in the previous place miss the spaciousness and service it provided; but, adapting to the altered venue, or knowing no different, a fresh clientele has emerged to frequent the new venue. The Central Park complex – café, ice rink and Gus the Gorilla's playground – even has its own gold loyalty card for frequent users.

Left and above: A couple of commemorative Poole Pottery plates designed by Dorset-based artist and illustrator Maria Burns. (Salisbury Photo Imaging Ltd)

Cool! A competitor in the Poole Park 1990 centenary marathon. (*Bournemouth Daily Echo*)

Centenary Celebrations (1890–1990)

In a lengthy lead-up to Poole Park's 100th birthday, council meetings, budgetary sub committees and the media debated many conflicting activities that might commemorate the event. When it was announced that roads would be resurfaced during the Spring Bank Holiday weekend 1990, the miniature-train operator Brian Merrifield and boat master Geoff Tapper were dismayed, anticipating the disruption would harm their trade by discouraging use of the park.

The Poole Carnival was resurrected after an absence of four years, and a carnival queen was crowned. Council architect Paul Hillman was responsible for restoring the splendid Norton's Gate.

The young Dorset-based artist and illustrator Maria Burns was commissioned to design a couple of commemorative plates which were produced by the prestigious Poole Pottery Co.

The popular annual Poole Marathon (established in 1986) was arranged to coincide with the celebrations. Prince Edward arrived on Saturday 30 June 1990 to witness the afternoon programme of youth activities.

Along most of the park's north and east boundaries the iron railings had been removed during the Second World War to be melted down, recycled, and made into munitions – although recently we have come to believe that much, if not all, of this architectural despoliation was never used but dumped. With them went a metal plate attached to an oak tree near the war memorial recording its planting by Princess Alice.

The existing replacements were installed for the park's 1990 centenary celebrations at a cost of £72,000. Anticipating Prince Edward's visit, it was proposed that they should be painted royal blue, but this was abandoned for what was considered a more dignified black and gold.

Children's Play Areas

It should be noted that children at play are not playing about; their games should be seen as their most serious-minded activity.
Michel Eyquem de Montaigne, French essayist, 1533–1592

Fablab opened on Sunday 20 May 1990 at a cost of £100,000. The first of its kind in the South of England, this commercial hands-on indoor science playground featured some forty mechanical, sonic and visual exhibitions, experiments and demonstrations. In the first year more than half a million visitors, including school parties, sampled its unique fusion of fun, fact and fantasy. Fablab lasted only three years, however, before it was replaced by something altogether more enduring.

When catering entrepreneur Adrian Forte and his wife Torfrida decided that there were few places to occupy their children, Carlotta aged two, and Lisa aged six, during wet weather, he did something about it and on Friday 14 May 1993, at 4.30 p.m., the town's mayor Bruce Grant-Braham opened their new indoor amenity. Gus the Gorilla's Jungle Playground was an early example of the indoor soft-play arenas, all plastic and primary colours, that are now familiar everywhere. Themed around a jungle clearing with areas for under fives and children up to the age of twelve (or, alternatively, not more than 150cm tall), it adjoined the Swan Lake/Cygnet/Central Park Café. This wonderland was created by top indoor-play designer Rupert Oliver of the Play Co. and cost South Coast Caterers Ltd (director, Adrian Forte) £80,000.

Above: The Cygnet play area, opened in 2005. (Geoffrey Budworth)

Left: The landmark 'falling-down tree'. (Geoffrey Budworth)

The attraction measuring 3,000sq.ft was set on three levels and had spiral, tube and drop slides, rope bridges and ladders, a huge ball pool, bouncers, a mini-maze, and interactive punch bags which screamed when hit.

At the start of 1995 the playground expanded by one-third, after £40,000 was spent on new equipment and safety systems, a parents-and-baby room and a special area exclusively for toddlers. Snacks or full meals, cold drinks, a cappuccino or something stronger (under the business's liquor license) were obtainable. As many as 100 children could occupy it at once. Gus the Gorilla's Jungle has something that Fablab had not, because it is still popular fifteen years later in 2008.

The swings, slides and seesaws for older children on the sloping West Field overlooking the main lake had been there for several decades when, on Saturday 12 November 2005, the Cygnet outdoor play area for three to twelve-year-olds was opened by the mayor. Railed off so as to be goose-free (see Wildfowl), close to the Central Park amenities and the miniature railway station, it was created by the council and the Friends of Poole Park, with £125,000 raised by central government grant and local donations so that it cost the local tax payer nothing.

It was an instant hit – despite cold weather – with young children, their parents and guardians. So popular was the 'talking tube' that it was quickly decided to duplicate it at the West Field site. Wear-and-tear from energetic usage is inevitable, along with some vandalism, but these are combated by continual 'stitch-in-time' repair and maintenance.

The 'Falling Down' Tree

A Corsican or black pine (*Pinus nigra 'maritima'*) has provided play and climbing opportunities for generations of children. In its native land it might grow to be 150ft tall but, exposed to coastal breezes in the park, this one fell over early in its life and grew along the grass-covered ground. Grandparents, who recall clambering on it themselves, saw their children do so, and now watch their grandchildren on this memorable park feature. There are actually several recumbent trees within the park that can be climbed upon but *the* 'falling down tree' is the one partially propped up beside the road on a piece of timber and it features in the logo of the Friends of Poole Park. (See also Trees, Shrubs and Plants)

CRIME AND LAW ENFORCEMENT

The primary object of an efficient police force is the prevention of crime.
Sir Richard Mayne, Metropolitan Police Commissioner, 1829

No doubt there was Victorian and Edwardian crime within the park, and perhaps prevention was no more or less effective in those days than now. The notorious 'sus' law (loitering with intent), now repealed, together with the offence of 'flashing' (indecent exposure), were both sixty-six years old in 1890. Fewer people used the newly opened park then, however, while spray-painted graffiti and drug trafficking by juveniles were unknown. Park keepers, gardeners and other grounds-men, as part of their duties, discouraged rowdies and ruffians. Adults in the park, too, may have felt better able to remonstrate, intervene and so thwart bad behaviour. Police constables in uniform patrolling on foot preserved the peace and reacted to offences … and prosecutions resulting in convictions incurred fines, imprisonment or both.

After both world wars, park usage burgeoned. The population was more mobile. Class distinctions were eroded. The demarcation between law and morality became blurred.

Policing the park has its pleasures. (Brian Merrifield)

Individual consciences became selective. People were more likely to take a shortcut across the cricket square, or feed the geese, despite notices asking them not to do so. Parking restrictions and motoring speed limits were treated by some drivers as irksome rules to be flouted.

Today, while peak-capped park keepers are defunct, the park is monitored by park rangers and site-specific CCTV surveillance that proved some litter, wrongly blamed on humankind, was actually scattered by agile foxes and squirrels raiding the litter bins. The Friends of Poole Park solved this by paying for hinged metal flaps to be fitted across the slots of these receptacles.

Byelaws

Byelaws are local laws made under an 'enabling' Act of Parliament, and those covering Poole Park are the Pleasure Grounds' Byelaws of 1875. Unfortunately they reflect their own era, dictating *inter alia* (as lawyers say) when you may, or may not, bring a goat into the park, and banning the beating or shaking of carpets and druggets. True, the speed limit for road vehicles was raised (in 1936) from 8mph to 15mph, and more recently to 20mph but the fine (once a swingeing £2) is now an affordable £20 ... and the authorities are powerless to act against those whose names and addresses cannot be ascertained.

The saltwater lake has been an occasional dumping ground for disparate items: a Wiltshire & Dorset bus taken from the nearby bus station (June 1983); a safe (September 1988); and a pillowcase stuffed with junk jewellery (November 2002).

Geoff Tapper's fleet of seventy-five boats was always a target for irresponsible youngsters. The compound where he kept the smaller paddle boats was broken into more than once and these craft used as ferries to the rowing boats moored offshore. Not content with free trips afloat, however, the miscreants often threw oars and rowlocks into the lake, and while oars floated and

The East Gate Lodge, with Superintendent Palmer and his dog Sauce commanding the carriageway. (Author's collection)

Park staff assembled in 1910, with Bonny the horse and Sauce the dog. (Andrew Hawkes)

might be retrieved later, the metal rowlocks or crutches (at £2 a pair, 1977 prices) sank and could not always be recovered from the muddy lake bed. In August 1982 one of his Canadian-style canoes valued at £180 was taken and recovered later washed up in Poole harbour.

Deliberate damage was worse. For instance, sometime after midnight on a Saturday in June 1989 vandals rolled a 2-cwt concrete waste bin to the lakeside, then lifted and launched the gigantic cylinder to crash down and sink a paddle boat moored alongside.

The zoo, surprisingly, had its share of thefts. In the night of Friday 7 May 1993, a thief forced an entry through an 8ft-high fence and stole two banded acaries (toucan-like birds distinguished by red stripes across their yellow breasts). Resale of these rare and microchipped creatures, which the zoo's management had bought only weeks earlier, could net the taker £700 each. A tortoise worth £150 was also stolen.

Later that year, on Sunday 12 September, a burglar took Wally, the salmon-crested cockatoo. Standing 18in tall, in various shades of pink, he was valued at £800 but might, keeper David Simmons suggested, have proved a handful for the thief (if male) as he was aggressive towards men, and also had a deafening squawk that could be heard a mile away.

Even minor crimes and misdemeanours can be costly. When the Friends of Poole Park agreed to affix simple bird boxes and feeders to trees, the park rangers had to recommend more expensive thief-proof models so as to foil any park visitor with larcenous intent and no conscience – the same individual, no doubt, who takes not only cuttings from the park's flowers and shrubs but the entire plants.

In 2006 a sonic repellent device known as a 'Mosquito' was acquired and installed in the vicinity of the Cygnet play area, programmed to transmit an intermittent stream of uncomfortable sound waves, audible only to the under-twenties, between 7 p.m. and midnight to deter youths from loitering there. The timing could be adjusted to take account of British Summer Time.

Despite the maker's assurance that the device causes no physical harm to its hearers, youth campaigners began in 2008 to agitate for these appliances be banned, as they demonized all youngsters indiscriminately, when effort ought to be devoted to seeking solutions for whatever social causes were leading to disaffected and disruptive young people.

DUCK POND

When the park was first laid out, this pond – smallest of the three expanses of water, but still sizeable – was also created. Surrounded by railings in an attempt to protect its inhabitants from foxes, this was the haunt of exotic species such as muscovy ducks and black swans whose wings had been clipped to prevent them from flying away.

In March 1983 Geoff Tapper had to hastily lug a dinghy from the boating lake, across the intervening road, and into the duck pond in response to a frantic report that a toddler's pushchair (with occupant) had toppled into the water and drifted out of reach. When retrieved, however, it contained only a doll and a bag of shopping … mum, granddad and toddler were still safe on land.

There is now a neat wooden A-frame duck house on each of its two island refuges for waterfowl, supplied in 2007 by the Friends of Poole Park.

One of the duck-pond islands and the A-frame bird shelter, which was erected in 2007. (Geoffrey Budworth)

The East Gate Lodge in 2007. (Geoffrey Budworth)

Entrances, Gates and Lodges

When we build, let us think that we build for ever.
John Ruskin, English author and art critic, 1818–1900

The park has five major gateways, all accessible to pedestrians: the East Gate, the Memorial Gate, Norton's Gate, Seldown Gate, and Whitecliff Road (located alongside the curiously named Twemlow Avenue). It also has at least nine other lesser gateways for those on foot, plus a pedestrian subway leading to and from the harbour-side area known as the Baiter. So the park is never closed. Traffic can use the entrances at East Gate (in only), Seldown Gate and Whitecliff Road (both two-way) but all three are closed to traffic during weekday mornings (6 a.m.–10 a.m.) to prevent the park being used as a short cut or rat run by workers heading to and from the town centre.

All three road entrances are enhanced by impressive brick and stone pillars inset with sea-life panels and topped with eagles and ornamental lamps. These terracotta embellishments were created by George Jenkins, a local potter who had previously been employed as chief sanitary engineer for the Great Exhibition in 1851.

East Gate

Located in the area known until the 1930s as 'Brown Bottom', this entrance has a neat single-story brick bungalow, built in 1888 to be occupied by one or other of the park keepers. These custodians, collectively know as 'parkies' in the early days included Superintendent Palmer, with his dog, Sauce, Messrs King, Prior (keeper), Hancock (foreman), Allen (general gardener), Dennitt, Shutler (boat proprietor), Dowder and Teague. One of their many and varied duties was to lock the gates at 9 p.m. in the summer and 6 p.m. in the winter, or alternatively at sunset whenever that occurred throughout the year.

On the north wall of the East Lodge is an ornamental terracotta plaque, in the form of a long scroll, describing how the park was donated to the town. Because it is never seen by drivers speeding past, and can be obscured with plant life, only those aware of its existence ever walk around the lodge to see it. The wording reads:

THIS LAND
CONSISTING OF 34 ACRES
WAS PRESENTED TO THE
CORPORATION
OF THE
TOWN AND COUNTY
OF THE
BOROUGH OF POOLE
FOR THE PURPOSES OF A
PUBLIC PARK
AND
RECREATION GROUND
FOR THE USE OF THE
INHABITANTS
IN PERPETUITY

BY THE
RIGHT HONOURABLE
BARON WIMBORNE
AND WAS
LAID OUT AT THE
PUBLIC EXPENSE
BY
JOHN ELFORD
BOROUGH SURVEYOR
1888
FRED^k STYRING
MAYOR

Norton's Gate

In the late 1960s the imposing gate pillars that had previously adorned the Norton's Gate entrance were taken down as part of an improved road and roundabout scheme, leaving only pedestrian access. The avenue of trees between the bowling and putting greens remained an important landscaped feature of the park, but minus the bandstand, built in 1889 when the park was laid out, upon which bands were paid by the council to play music on high days and holidays to public sunbathing in deckchairs.

This gate was named in memory of Victorian philanthropist John James Norton, a self-made timber magnate (for him money really did grow on trees), who ranks as one of Poole's most famous citizens.

It was restored as part of the park's centenary celebrations, when Christchurch designer-craftsman David Ballantyne, head of ceramics at Bournemouth College, created the two replica terracotta eagles that now surmount the replacement gate pillars.

Seldown Gate

Built in 1888 at the same time as the East Gate Lodge, this larger building (with a cart house and a stable block at the rear) was occupied by the first gatekeeper Albert Saville until his death in 1907. On the side of the building facing out onto Kingland Road, beneath the gable, is a round, stone coat of arms predating the one now used by the corporation (see Sundries).

At the front of the building with its red bricks and stone quoins, on the left-hand gable, is a shield bearing the date AD 1888, and there is a tablet affixed to the wall on the left of the front door with the inscription:

THIS
PARK
WAS OPENED BY
HIS ROYAL HIGHNESS
ALBERT EDWARD
PRINCE OF WALES
ON
JANUARY, 18th 1890

MAYOR
PHILIP EDWARD LIONEL BUDGE

The lodge's 'secret' scroll. (Geoffrey Budworth)

The borough's civic offices overlooks the park's East Gate. (Geoffrey Budworth)

The restored Norton's Gate. (Geoffrey Budworth)

One of the eagles atop the Norton's Gate pillars. (Geoffrey Budworth)

Seldown Lodge with date stone. (Geoffrey Budworth)

Victorian coat of arms. (Geoffrey Budworth)

The date stone on the front of the building. (Geoffrey Budworth)

Commemorative tablet.
(Geoffrey Budworth)

Above and below: Public toilets, heritage style, built in the 1980s. (Geoffrey Budworth)

Above and below: The Whitecliff Gate entrance in the 1890s and in 2007. (Geoffrey Budworth)

Above left and right: The keyhole bridge. (Geoffrey Budworth)

A pedestrian gate. (Geoffrey Budworth)

SHERIFF
CHRISTOPHER HILL, JUN.

ALDERMEN
[six names are listed]

COUNCILLORS
[eighteen names are listed]
HENRY SALTER DICKENSON, TOWN CLERK
JOHN ELFORD, C.E., BOROUGH SURVEYOR

PUBLIC LAVATORIES

This compact brick building appears contemporary with the Seldown Gatehouse, but it is actually a commendable reproduction job opened as recently as February 1985. It is also a praiseworthy recycling enterprise, the roof tiles and the railings atop the wall having both been salvaged from a demolished school building close by the Seldown entrance.

WHITECLIFF ROAD GATE

This gate close by Twemlow Avenue is used by drivers heading from or to the keyhole bridge that penetrates the railway embankment. The terracotta sea-life panels decorating its brick pillars were unearthed by workers digging to restore Norton's Gate and relocated here.

THE KEYHOLE BRIDGE

Built by the railway company to take a horse and carriage, this pinch point reduces motor vehicles to a single alternate line, first-come-first-served, as they enter or leave the park. The narrowest of kerbs enables pedestrians to keep off the carriageway. Traffic lights would be preferable, but anyway it is an informal limit to car speeds and a bar to bigger vehicles.

FASHIONS

We still buy cotton frocks in April as a folk magic to bring on summer, forgetting that the golden afternoon of the Edwardian era was due, as much as anything, to the fact that they never (well almost never), abandoned their petticoats and stays and waistcoats.
Katherine Whitehorn, journalist and columnist, the *Observer*, 7 August 1966

In 1890 many a smartly attired boy, as he outgrew his toddler's dress (that's right, boys in dresses), was put into knickerbockers or short trousers, before a suit. This progression was eliminated by the arrival of affordable ready-to-wear clothing, two of the new styles being a sailor suit and a 'Norfolk' suit. Some girls too wore sailor suits. Children from poorer homes wore shoddier imitations and hand-me-down mixtures, very often with boots.

Girls with better-off parents were dressed according to the aspirations of their mothers, many retaining the flounces and frilly femininity of an earlier era, while older emancipated females entering the workplace adopted the more mannish shapes and fabrics of the 'New Woman' typist, secretary or teacher.

A boy in a sailor suit, 1919. Note the Edwardian teahouse in background. (Author's collection)

Moonlit assignations (with rhymes reminiscent of pre-Second World War Bournemouth author and poet Cumberland Clark). (Andrew Hawkes)

On Sunday afternoons a stroll in the park was an activity for maturing young people of both sexes, as well as their elders, to feed the swans on the lakes or the peacocks and pheasants in the bird sanctuary. The more energetic might walk around the lake by way of the footpath beside the railway embankment. This was done in their best Sunday clothes. One man recalls how, aged eighteen, he paraded around town and park wearing a blue pinstripe suit and a bowler hat (swapped in summer for a straw boater) while carrying a walking cane with a silver knob. Girls would strive to be elegantly dressed, with a new bonnet purchased for Easter.

Sailor suits did not last long into the twentieth century. Styles and materials evolved. As riding in motorcars or on motorcycle pillions replaced strolling, boaters, bowlers and bonnets disappeared. 'Flappers' wore shorter skirts and bobbed hair. By the 1920s and early '30s, informality was apparent. Blazers and Fair Isle jumpers crossed over from sporting wear to everyday use. Belts replaced braces.

From 1942, until some time after the end of hostilities, wartime utility regulations restricted both the cut and size of boys' clothing. Teenage youths were kept in short trousers, as the cheap alternative by their parents to long flannel trousers with turn-ups, for as long as possible. Then, during the 1950s the influence of American films – lumber jackets, T-shirts and jeans – led to a youth revolution in marketing that continues today with young people more style and fashion conscious than their parents.

What was worn beneath outer garments in the early twentieth century in Poole Park might be gleaned from retailers' advertisements of the time. This was less irksome for boys than for girls with their corset bodices and the later 'Liberty' bodices. However, from the onset of the First World War, dresses became shorter. By the 1920s the gymslip was the appropriate outfit for schoolgirls. After the austerity of the Second World War, Dior's 'New Look', the marriage of Princess Elizabeth in 1947, and her Coronation as Queen in 1953, all had an influence upon female fashions. At this time the mandatory wearing of hats (girls and boys) had largely disappeared, except with certain school uniforms, and as a badge of peer group recognition.

From buttoned-up Edwardian style to laid-back Lycra leisurewear and logos, we dress differently now.

FOUNTAIN

Whatever it is, I fear the Greeks even when they bring gifts.
Virgil, Roman poet, 70–19BCE

On Friday 8 June 1990, Lord Wimborne, together with his second wife Lady Venetia, made his first visit to Poole Park since inheriting the title twenty-three years earlier. The couple flew in from Paris where he lived as a tax exile (said to be worth £25 million), although he still owned about 1,900 acres of the Canford Estates in the Poole area. As great-grandson of the first Lord Wimborne, who donated the land for the park, he had come to present the town with a nineteenth-century French-style fountain. After visiting the mayor's parlour, the distinguished guests were taken to the park in a horse-drawn carriage to unveil the fountain in front of Mayor Ann Stribley and her Sheriff, Doreen Bugo, where Lord Wimborne made a speech.

It would prove to be a costly gift. Lord and Lady Wimborne had donated £30,000 to buy the structure but the borough were then compelled to lay out around £60,000 for its installation. Councillors, alarmed at the possible reaction of local tax payers, were particularly angry over a

Above and left: The costly fountain. (Author's collection)

£9,000 internal fee from the engineer's department for design of the equipment and surround for the fountain, which included underwater lighting.

Within weeks of the switch on, pranksters poured detergent into the water creating a basinful of soap suds which blew on the breeze in frothy airborne blobs, to the amusement of some passers-by and the irritation of others.

But it seems to have attracted no more vandalism than any other piece of public sculpture, until in, 1994, the police caught youngsters trying to rip the concrete lions from their pedestals, but could only caution them because of their age. Local stonemason Dan Churchill on more than one occasion had to repair the 24in-high beasts. On another occasion four thoughtless youths damaged the ornamental wall that surrounds the fountain by skateboarding on it.

FRESHWATER LAKE

When a road was built along the east side of the saltwater lake, it cut off a muddy area of swamp fed by one or two existing springs. This was then dug out to create a leg-of-mutton-shaped freshwater lake. The narrow angle was crossed by a rustic bridge of timber handrails and intertwined branches which, after its destruction by enemy action during the Second World War (see Wartime), was replaced by the more functional one that today carries not only pedestrians but the miniature railway track and trains too.

In September 1983 a park user reported that she had seen at least four ducks dragged down beneath the surface of the water, never to reappear, leaving only a few feathers on the surface. Their nemesis was probably a killer pike seen by other witnesses who estimated it was 2ft long. Experts believe it could have been put into the lake, but more likely had washed down a watercourse when younger and smaller.

In the autumn of 1985, fifty years of accumulated silt was dredged from the bottom of the enclosure, eroded and collapsed banks were restored, and the water's edge was relined with Purbeck stone. This clean up took two months during which time, surprisingly, no rare artefacts or antique curiosities were recovered (only an old bicycle).

In 1989 several ducks were killed by a rare avian type C botulism toxin, and in September/October 1991 another outbreak occurred. It was caused, experts thought, when the bacterium had favourable conditions to multiply due to rotting leaves and bread on the bottom and sides of the lake being exposed by six weeks of very dry weather. The risk to humans was small, barring infection via deep cuts or open wounds, and the saltwater lake was unaffected. When it rained, and water levels rose again, there were not further waterfowl casualties.

MINIATURE RAILWAY

Small is beautiful.
E.F. Schumacher, German-born economic consultant, 1911–1977

When the Second World War ended engineer George Vimpany, using skills acquired in a Southampton factory constructing Spitfire fighter planes, built the replica steam locomotive *Vanguard* (No. 1001), first of the Atlantic class 4-4-2 locomotives. Weighing two tons, and 13ft 6in long, it took him sixteen months to complete and was finished in 1947 at the considerable cost of just over £2,000. He also built a set of six coaches.

The rustic bridge. (Author's collection)

George Vimpany ready to haul his first passenger load with steam locomotive *Vanguard* on Easter Saturday, 9 April 1949. (Brian Merrifield)

Comedy, it's a serious business – Ronnie Barker and Ronnie Corbett, with a bearded Brian Merrifield. (Brian Merrifield)

Filming the anarchic, award-winning Liverpudlian comic, actor and writer Alexei Sayle. (Brian Merrifield)

Brian test-walks *Arthur* around the track. (Brian Merrifield)

Moving to Poole, he next sought permission to build a model steam railway by approaching the council who, after the dreariness and uncertainties of the Second World War, happened to be keen on transforming the town into a holiday resort. So in 1948, despite the apprehension of some locals about harm to peace, tranquillity and wildfowl by such a development, the corporation decided to locate his proposed railway in Poole Park. They also agreed to construct an engine and equipment shed costing £150, together with a bridge to replace the earlier one destroyed by a stray German bomb (see Wartime) costing another £150.

George began track-laying towards the end of that year – learning as he laid it – encircling the freshwater lake with about ¾ mile of 10¼in gauge track made with 12 tons of rail he had been lucky to obtain a licence from the Ministry of Supply to buy, as post-war rationing in Britain extended to raw materials. The council helped with a heap of ballast.

Pending the removal of *Vanguard* to Poole, George cleverly persuaded Portsmouth's local Standard 'Vanguard' car dealer to display his locomotive in the car showroom.

The railway began operating within the park on Saturday 9 April 1949 in time for the Easter holiday. The weather was exceptionally hot and the train was packed until nightfall. The mayor was invited to the official opening, but declined, ostensibly due to another engagement. In fact he was opposed to the train and had been the only member of the park's committee to vote against the resolution to allow it. For the rest of the summer it remained popular, people often standing in line for an hour to have their rides, but post-war austerity had conditioned them to queuing and amusements were fewer then.

The original agreement signed by the council and George Vimpany prohibited the train's operation on Sundays, but this ban was soon lifted and written permission given to operate (and use the train's whistle) up to 10.30 p.m.

Prior to raising steam …

… then away they go! (Both Brian Merrifield)

Brian Merrifield driving modernised diesel loco D1000. (Brian Merrifield)

The magnificent *Chiltern Shuttle*. (Brian Merrifield)

Chris Bullen, miniature train boss, sponsors a new traffic-warning sign. During the photo-shoot an elderly man drove his car through the wooden ducks, knocking them down and scattering them, then continued on, apparently unaware of what he had done. (*Bournemouth Daily Echo*)

The cost of a ticket was 1*s.* for an adult and 6*d.* for a child, with the corporation claiming twenty-five per cent of all takings. These fares remained the same for twenty years. Then, in 1969, they began to rise as wages, insurance and the new Selective Employment Tax all added to running costs. At the time of writing the fare is £1 for each passenger which, allowing for currency devaluation (1967), decimalisation (1972), VAT (1973), increased fuel costs and inflation (both ongoing), is probably the equivalent more or less of what it was when the railway first ran in 1949.

As bank loans were costly and hard to arrange, with credit unthinkable, George Vimpany looked for a sleeping partner to put money into the venture. George Lawrence was a shrewd choice, as he was a local coal merchant who supplied fuel for the locomotive. Together they traded as Southern Miniature Railways Ltd (SMR). George's wife Beryl assisted too, with administration and ticket sales, and every Saturday helped him push the heavy locomotive from its shed to the water tap at the station for a weekly boiler flush through. Not until 1960 was she freed from this chore, when the petrol-driven locomotive D7000 was commissioned and could shunt *Atlantic* to the station. This was built locally, the body and chassis in the Poole Park engine shed. The gearbox and engine fittings emerged from Longfleet Engineering Works (opposite the landmark Shah of Persia public house). In 1990/91 it was converted to diesel.

George also built another steam locomotive, *Victory*.

An early problem was flooding when strong south-west winds caused the saltwater lake to slop over the intervening road and footpath and wash away the track ballast. So the council rebuilt and realigned both, raising them 12in to 15in; and, at the same time, the SMR took the opportunity to redirect the track away from the path and to elevate that section by about 9in.

The SMR's operating licence expired in December 1953 and a new licence was granted for a further five years with the same conditions, but with a controversial extra clause to pay the local business rate of tax, which in March 1954 was assessed to be £150 a year. The council appealed on the ground that the railway was an amenity and so not liable to rates; alternatively, if that argument failed, that the assessment was too high. In April 1956 an intractable valuation office responded, raising its demand by 666 per cent to £1,000 a year. The SMR itself now instructed solicitors. Not until June 1959 did the Land Tribunal rule that the railway was not rateable, when the town clerk and the borough treasurer refused to refund George and his partner, the £729 15s. that had been dutifully paid during the five years of appeal proceedings, offering to reimburse only £150

Fortunately the summer of 1959 was dry and abnormally hot and takings were the best since the railway began ten years earlier. In 1957 George had added the boating concession on the saltwater lake to his business activity and so, as the renewal of this licence would run until 31 December 1964, the council agreed to renew his railway operating licence until the same date.

The demolition of the old Edwardian tearooms and the construction of a replacement to open at Whitsun 1961 (see Catering) necessitated the demolition of the existing railway station and a new one to be built nearby, with some alteration to the existing track, so as not to obstruct the panoramic view from the new café/restaurant.

The miniature railway station was originally named 'Poole', but the council were concerned that people wanting to go by rail to London (Waterloo) might turn up with their luggage at George's SMR version by mistake and asked him to rename it 'Poole Park', which he did.

In 1965, when the operating licence was yet again due for renewal, council officers claimed that the smoke, ash and dirt from the steam engines marred other amenities within the park, backing up this dubious assertion with more realistic concerns about the safety of the steam boilers, their operation, maintenance and inspection. While, as far as George was concerned, coal was becoming costly and difficult to obtain, and it was a tedious task breaking up five 15-gallon oil drums of the stuff every day into pieces small enough to fit the engines' fire boxes. So he agreed to phase out steam locos, the licence was renewed for a further seven years, and daily steam trains stopped running at the end of the 1965 season, with only occasional steam events to be held until 1969.

In a letter of complaint to the town clerk dated May 1969, an agitated complainant described how, while visitors to the park were feeding the ducks, 'the train dashed through and killed one'. The writer and others 'stared in horror' and all that could be seen were 'white feathers and white faces'. In fact it was a pigeon which, lured onto the track by bread thrown from the occupants of a parked car, narrowly escaped the engines wheels and merely lost a few tail feathers.

George Vimpany, with help from his family, owned and operated the model railway for thirty years – and the boating concession for twenty-one years – until he retired due to ill health in 1978, during which time it was estimated his trains carried a total at least 5 and maybe 6 million passengers.

At this juncture the council decided to uncouple the railway and boat-operating licences and, re-examining the small print of both, noticed belatedly that they had an obligation to enclose the entire railway track with a 3ft-high paling fence as part of their duty of care to park users under the Occupiers' Liability Act 1957, because the trains ran on land over which the public wandered unchecked and unguarded. Park users protested that such a fence would also enclose the entire freshwater lake, blocking access to the water's edge and the waterfowl. When if ever, they queried, had anyone come off worst in conflict with a moving train? So the fencing clause was deleted from the renewed licences, as was the need for fire insurance because the risk to trackside vegetation was reduced now that coal-fired steam engines were no longer used.

On Tuesday 9 October 1979 the railway was transferred to Geoff Tapper (see Boating) who took on a partner. Brian Merrifield was Geoff's brother-in-law, a qualified and experienced motor and classic motor-cycle mechanic, who had only recently moved to Wrexham in North Wales but was willing to sell up and return to Poole. The two men quickly settled into their new venture, with Geoff concentrating on the boats and Brian (assisted by his wife Nicola) running and maintaining the railway under the revised name of Southern Miniature Railways.

When the Parks Department advised Brian that the track would have to be realigned during the winter of 1980/81 so that they could landscape the adjacent banks of the freshwater lake, he replaced both original track and sleepers which had been in use since 1948 (when they were second hand). It was neither cheap nor easy to obtain suitable materials and, to offset the cost of the rails, he used seasoned timber sleepers, but these had to be replaced after a few years with the steel ones which remain in use today.

On Good Friday, 1982, a film featuring the Two Ronnies (comedians Barker and Corbett) called *By the Sea* was shown on BBC television. It featured a scene on the Poole Park railway, in which Ronnie Barker and a very large lady were crammed into one of the carriages (specially constructed by boat-builder Geoff Tapper for the purpose). The comedian Alexei Sayle was also filmed on the railway in 1990 for his programme *Alexei Sayle's Stuff*. In December 1993 the television presenter and actor Matthew Kelly rode with Father Christmas on a train to open a Christmas fair within the park and in 1995 the Poole & Parkstone Musical Theatre Society used little steam locomotive *Arthur* and train as part of the publicity for their show *The Rhythm of Life*.

The name Poole Park Railway was adopted in 1986. Then, in 1989 Brian and Geoff amicably decided to separate – Geoff to concentrate solely on the boating franchise, leaving Brian with the railway, once he could raise the cash to buy out Geoff's interest in it.

Diesel had replaced steam in 1969, after which the licence for the miniature railway forbade steam engines but, as ticket sales fell, the corporation's amenities committee agreed to their reintroduction. So in November 1991 the saddle-tank engine *Arthur* was purchased by Brian 'for the price of an extremely good car' from the Royal Victoria Country Park at Netley, near Southampton. *Arthur*, built in the early 1980s at Selby, Yorkshire, by Jack Huddell, was modelled on a 1901 vintage British Coal Board locomotive by Chapman & Furneaux named *Holmside*, from an 0-6-0 design by Martin Evans, published in *Model Engineer*.

The locomotive was used only infrequently for special events during summer months, and occasionally out of season, as it was too expensive and labour intensive for everyday use. In 1998 Brian sold *Arthur* and reinvested the money from the sale in the existing operation. *Lion* also enjoyed its final outing towards the close of 1995, after which it too was sold. Park regulars may remember steam reappearing briefly around that time in the form of the chunky *Tinkerbell* locomotive.

May Day 1995 saw the official launch of the Friends of Poole Park Railway (founder member: Roger Sansom) whose aims were to lend support and raise funds to celebrate the success of the railway's half-century in 1999, and to ensure its survival. The ceremony was performed in the presence of a large number of supporters and enthusiasts by Poole's Deputy Mayor, Cllr Bernard Ewart, who cut a cake baked, and suitably decorated with an image of D7000 for the occasion, by Roger's wife Liz.

D7000 had an all-or-nothing clutch that, wrong footed, could easily stall the engine. When that happened, it had to be turned over with a starting handle poked into its rear end, but only after the train of carriages had been detached and the engine pushed to a straight section of track. This was because the cam shaft was mounted on the bogie wheels and had to be aligned to receive the handle. Brian recalls one occasion when, having contrived to do this (uncoupling, recoupling, pushing), only to stall the engine again and again, he finally got going to a round of applause from the passengers.

In 1996 the magnificent American 'Switcher' steam locomotive *Chiltern Shuttle* was loaned to the park by Watford Railway, but, despite this and other initiatives, by 1997 ticket sails had fallen from 180,000 (two-thirds children, one-third adults) to 60,000.

In April 2005 Brian Merrifield sold the railway to Chris Bullen, who already owned and operated the colourful road train running around Poole town on pneumatic tyres between the park and the town quay. Chris had plans for a new 'steam-effect' locomotive, easier access for disabled children and seasonal events such as a children's zoo at Easter and the conversion of the engine shed into Santa's grotto at Christmas. While intent on realising an entrepreneurial profit, he was also heard to say; 'I look upon my job as being the custodian of a piece of Poole history.'

In 2009 Poole Park miniature railway will attain its Diamond Jubilee after sixty years of continuous operation.

MODEL YACHT CLUB

Small but perfectly formed.
Duff Cooper, 1st Viscount Norwich, British diplomat and author, 1890–1954

Soon after Poole Park opened, in 1890, a model-yacht regatta was held on the saltwater lake and, from the dates inscribed on surviving trophies and medals from the period, it is evident that as early as 1900, a model yacht and boat club was established in the south-east corner adjacent to the keyhole bridge. Arthur Vincent Shutler (see Boating) not only made and donated a rowing boat to the club, to recover models becalmed out of reach, but was an active and successful competitor (and so presumably an adept model-yacht builder too).

The Poole & District Model Yacht Club re-emerged after the First World War, although early records are believed to have been destroyed in a fire. Model sail boats at that time were controlled by self-steering vanes attached to their rudders, and would continue to sail away across the lake on the preset tack – unless somehow turned back onto a reciprocal course. So handling them necessitated not only a skipper but another crew member who, from the lengthy catwalk that encloses the club's roughly rectangular portion of lake, could reach out with a pole to return or retrieve boats. The dilapidated wooden walkway pictured in a 1921 magazine photograph was destroyed by gales in 1923, when the corporation was unable to afford the cost of replacement, after which club races must have been haphazard events.

The club became extinct again at the outbreak of the Second World War (1939–1945) when trophies were sold to cover its debts.

In 1950 the Poole Yacht & Power Boat Club was started, and by 1953 members had a new and larger clubhouse. The corporation then spent around £2,000 to replace the old wooden

Above and below: The catwalk can seem redundant … but it shelters the yachting lagoon in its lee from blustery winds and choppy water. (Geoffrey Budworth)

Radio-controlled 'A'-class model yachts vie at the start of the 2006 National Championships. (Poole Radio Yacht Club: Commodore, Derek White)

A typical Saturday club race with the fast little Laser class. (Poole Radio Yacht Club: Commodore, Derek White)

catwalk with the concrete one that now encloses the estimated 11,000sq.m of water leased by the club. The handrails and supporting stanchions of galvanized-iron pipe, about 240m long, were added thirty years later in January 1983 at a cost to the council of £11,600.

When boat storage adjoining the club house burned down, the opportunity was taken to rebuild it with a raised ceiling to accommodate boats that, standing upright, from weighted keels to aluminium or carbon-fibre mast tops, can be around 3m tall.

In the late 1950s some members began experimenting with radio-controlled craft. Colonel Bowden owned a model shop in Westover Road, Bournemouth; Tommy Grant owned another in Charminster Road and George Honnest-Redlich was well known in the world of model aircraft. The first transmitters together with their HT batteries were so big and expensive that one set was housed in a redundant 'stop-me-and-buy-one' Wall's ice-cream tricycle. The club held its first national radio-controlled (RC) yacht regatta in 1959.

RC yachting was only truly launched when small and light transistors replaced the clumsy and less reliable glass-thermionic valves, and 27MHz digital equipment became readily available, after which single-handed sailors operating on individual radio-frequency wavelengths could undertake races around buoyed courses. Single-handed control is achieved by means of radio-frequency signals that cause mini motors within the yachts to whir and alter the angle of the rudder, while tiny winches haul in or pay out the running rigging, enabling the boats to tack and gybe, to beat to windward, to reach, or to run (sometimes goose-winged) before a following breeze.

For several years the club sailed both RC and vane-controlled boats, but vane sailing eventually died out, and in 1983 the club's name was changed to Poole Radio Yacht Club to reflect this mutation. The park became a popular venue for the national championships of the Model Yacht Association (MYA) and some open events attracted entrants from overseas.

The four essential elements required for model yachting are: technical (design and build); tweaking (setting up the standing rigging); trimming (sails); and tactical (wind awareness and course selection). These four T's are practised and polished assiduously by the almost exclusively male membership that pursues an apparently serene pastime – which, at its most competitive, is actually as calculated as chess and as cruel as croquet.

Members are a hardy lot who can be found waterside and sailing not only in balmy weather but also in raw blows and chilling temperatures. While some canny helmsmen are adept at ghosting along in light airs, other skippers only perform well when thrashing along in rougher conditions. There are those who always sail to win, leaving astern anyone content with a more leisurely rate of knots. Some boats too are cruisers, others thoroughbred racers.

Apart from the energy consumed in making and operating these models, the sailboats are eco-friendly playthings that cut silently through the water, which heals up astern of them, leaving not a trace of their passing.

In 1994, responding to members' wishes, the club added a section for devotees of scale boats other than MYA racing classes. Any model is welcomed that is driven primarily by sail power, for example: Thames barges, Bristol Channel pilot cutters, and square-rigged men-o'-war. About one third of the members from time to time join in mixed relay races between teams sailing both racing boats and scale craft.

There are a few electric-powered scale craft (but none propelled by an internal combustion engine), generally second boats of sailing-craft owners.

On a Sunday afternoon in August 2000 the club celebrated fifty years under its current name, with an invitation to the Portsmouth Model Display Team, when several hundred spectators gathered around the model boating enclosure to watch two battles re-enacted. In one, seventeenth-century galleons exchanged cannon fire with an island fortress and in the other U-boats raided a convoy of merchantmen and sank an oil tanker.

The Poole Yacht & Power Boat Club's members are mostly male and aged around sixty. Its future depends upon recruitment and retention of younger replacements for those older hands who are ultimately reaching their voyages' ends. It is to be hoped that the club does endure, as it gives pleasure not only to devotees of model boating but to all park users who pause and watch the make-believe boats on their make-believe sea.

PAGEANT

It's all part of life's rich pageant.
                    Arthur Marshall, British writer and broadcaster, 1910–1989

In 1952 the council went ahead with a proposal from the Honourable Mrs FitzGerald, owner of the Fitz Club in classy Canford Cliffs village, for a Poole pageant and the pre-eminent female open-air event director Gwen Lally was commissioned to stage it. Poole historian H.P. Smith, agreed to write the libretto, assisted by historical novelist Miss Margaret Scott. Miss Elizabeth Gifford produced three ballets for the performance. Mr B.G. Hillier was appointed the project's business manager, and proceeds would go to the Disabled Sailors' and Soldiers' Aid Society.

The result was an outdoor performance of nine episodes in Poole's history, from the Roman invasion of Hamworthy in AD 44, to the opening of Poole Park by the Prince of Wales in 1890, all linked with commentary from 'Old Harry' (the sea-girt limestone pillar located off the southernmost tip of the Isle of Purbeck) who was supposed to have witnessed it all from his vantage beyond the harbour entrance.

Over 1,500 locals volunteered to play various roles, as mortals or mythical sea nymphs, peasants or nobles. John Valentine of the Society of Poole Men grew a beard to appear as Edward, Prince of Wales (and kept it for the rest of his life). Many council members and town-hall staff took part, led by Town Clerk Wilson Kenyon and his wife, in (unprecedented) civic robes and regalia. The West Field end of Poole Park was enclosed, stands were erected to hold up to 2,000 spectators, and an adjoining area of the saltwater lake was roped off. Advertising banners were displayed over the entrances to the park.

On the opening night, Monday 4 August, twenty mayors from nearby towns added pomp to a full house as a fanfare of trumpets and a peel of thunder preceded Old Harry's greeting and prologue delivered in authentic Dorset dialect by the well-known radio personality Ralph Wightman. This narration on other evenings would be performed by G.W. Skeggs. As the start had been delayed by bad weather – although the power cut feared as part of the Electricity Board's power-shedding programme never occurred – it was late when Old Harry delivered his farewell address.

The pageant closed on 16 August. Gwen Lally died in 1963 and her autographed cue book for the Poole Pageant is now in the matchless collection of rare items owned by local historian Andrew Hawkes.

Above and below: Medieval capers at the Poole Pageant, 1952. (Andrew Hawkes)

Royal Occasions

If you have a Royal Family you have to make the best of whatever personalities the genetic lottery comes up with.

Professor Ben Pimlott, British historian, 1945–2004

1897

Queen Victoria's Diamond Jubilee was celebrated in the park with a roast dinner for the town's children, and timber magnate G.F. Norton, augmented his earlier donation of a library to the town with an adjacent gymnasium.

1902

The late Queen Victoria's eldest son Albert was crowned King Edward VII, having served a sixty-year apprenticeship in the role, and his belated succession was marked within the park by dinner and tea for children and old folk.

1911

Following the death of King Edward VII in 1910, his successor King George V's Coronation the following 22 June generated more ambitious celebrations within the park, presided over by the Mayor of Poole, Cllr Joseph Alfred Hawkes.

The day had begun badly when the carriage carrying elderly residents from the Hamworthy Almshouses caught one of its wheels in the railway lines. The wheel broke, tipping the passengers out. Apart from being shocked and shaken, however, nobody was badly hurt.

The town was decorated with flags and bunting, and, although at least one report of the occasion mentions heavy rain and gales, from outside the Guildhall a gathering of mayoral councillors, territorial forces, a lifeboat crew, fire brigade, police and friendly societies marched in procession to St James' Church for Divine Service. Afterwards they all went to the park where dinner was provided for the town's 'Aged Inhabitants'.

At the end of dinner, the borough's children aged between four and fifteen years old assembled near the summer house at the West Field end and were addressed by the mayor (although not all could hear what he said). Each was given a small tin of chocolates with a picture of the new King and Queen on the lid and Coronation mugs made by Dorset Pottery from local red clay with the Royal personages' heads embossed on the front and decorated with yellow clay slip.

The young people then walked in procession through the park where afternoon sports and races were held. These included cycling around the track, a two-mile walking race, a one-mile handicap cycle-carrier race for errand boys, greasy pole, rowing and children's events including a sack race, wheelbarrow race, skipping and hopping, after which there was tea for all.

Later in the evening a military torchlight tattoo was held which ended with lighting a bonfire on the distant viewpoint at Constitutional Hill. (A handsomely printed official programme commemorating the Silver Jubilee of George V records all of the above.)

1935

Three days of celebrations in May marked the Silver Jubilee of King George V and Queen Mary. There was a royal salute of twenty-one maroons, band concerts, sports, maypole dancing and illuminations. All pensioners aged seventy or over and any unemployed over eighteen were paid the munificent sum of 2*s*. 6*d*.

Mayor Joseph Alfred Hawkes lauds Coronation Day in 1911. (Geoffrey Budworth)

1937

On Wednesday 12 May, the Coronation of King George VI, a mock up of the Loch Ness Monster created by Poole Amateur Rowing Club appeared on the boating lake. Buoyed up by 10-gallon oil drums, the 124ft-long serpentine creature weighed 3½ tons. Stuffed with combustible materials and fireworks it was set alight, with the aid of petrol and paraffin after several hours of heavy rain earlier, and burned spectacularly to the delight of an assembled crowd.

1953

Poole's first female mayor, Margaret Mary Llewellin (serving her second term of office) led the town's celebrations for the Coronation of Queen Elizabeth II on Tuesday 2 June. In the park itself these began with a fanfare by the Parkstone Sea Training School Band and a loyal address. A procession of uniformed armed and auxiliary services assembled at the Middle Gate and marched to the cricket pavilion, where a short religious service was held with hymns sung to accompaniment by the local Salvation Army corps.

The afternoon saw athletics, cycling, rowing and other aquatic sports that included a model-yacht regatta. The new-fangled radio-controlled yacht signals were disrupted by bad weather, so some conventional vane-steered sailing was resorted to, and the scale-model *Black Prince* steamed up and down the length of the lagoon. The Royal Corps of Signals renowned motorcycle display team put on a show, as did the fire brigade.

In the evening audiences were entertained with all sorts of dancing (tap, ballet, musical comedy, rhythmic). A swimming gala was held in the open-air pool, with a water-polo game advertised for afterwards (if there was time). Each schoolchild was presented with a Coronation mug decorated with an image of the Queen and the council's coat of arms. The entire day overran its budgeted cost of £2,504 by £126 (5 per cent).

Celebrations culminated with planting an American blue cedar tree (*Cedrus Atlantica glauca*) in Copse Close. (The commemorative programme cost a silver sixpence.)

1988

On the morning of Wednesday 14 September, a radiant Diana, Princess of Wales landed in the park by helicopter for a two-hour visit to lend her support to the 'Light up a Life' campaign for sick children.

1989

Mid-morning on Thursday 30 November, Anne, the Princess Royal, also arrived by helicopter for a visit to the HQ of the RNLI in her capacity as President of the Missions to Seamen.

2002

For the Golden Jubilee of Queen Elizabeth's accession to the throne on the death of her father George VI in 1952, the massive 'Party @ the Park' was held on Monday 3 June, which despite the rain that has occasionally complicated Poole's outdoor events, contrived to have live music, entertainments, games and family fun.

SALTWATER LAKE

I hear lake water lapping, with low sounds by the shore.
W.B. Yeats, Irish poet and Nobel Prize winner, 1865–1939

When the London & South Western Railway Co. extended its track from Bournemouth to link up with the Dorchester line, they build an embankment from Whitecliff across the shallow water of Parkstone Bay. In June 1885, announcing its intention to duplicate the railway line, the company asked if the council would require a tidal opening to the isolated area of water behind the embankment. The council replied that they planned to maintain this area as an ornamental lake and would therefore need a channel about 8ft wide by 8ft high (2.4m by 2.4m).

In February the following year tenders were received for the construction of tidal gates to control the flow of water through this channel (now known as 'the bunny') between the lake and the harbour, the successful tender coming from the Dorset Foundry Co. in the sum of £172 10s. 0d. These sluice gates, when opened, allowed the harbour's tidal waters to flow in and out, the level and depth of the saltwater lake rising and falling accordingly. This was intended to drain the lake, although it did so only partially. Writing to the *Poole Herald* newspaper more than once, Mr Harker Curtis (see Traffic) contended that the gates were hung upside down. When closed, as they were most of the time, the saltwater lake was maintained at a depth of around 4ft (1.2m). This made it safe for a variety of craft to be hired out to paying public (see Boating).

During the pre-1890 planning enquiries with solicitors acting for Lord Wimborne, the town clerk for the Borough of Poole did his best to safeguard the use of the lake by taking a licence from the Crown Commissioners and obtaining a lease from Lord Wimborne of such rights as he might yet possess over it, on a ninety-nine-year lease, at a cost of 1s. per annum. Sixty years later, in 1951, after an indecisive interview with the then viscount at which the corporation offered to purchase these rights, the freehold of the lake area was compulsorily purchased by the council, for the benefit of Poole inhabitants, for the small sum of £480.

ALGAE

One summer in the mid-1950s lorry loads of dead fish had to be removed from the saltwater lake, killed apparently during hot, dry weather when a growth of unidentified marine organism

Flotilla of waterfowl and the distant Purbeck Hills. (Geoffrey Budworth)

formed a film on the surface of the water and deprived them of oxygen. The remedy was to open the sluices and let the lake fill and empty with the tides during the winter. At around this time the sluice gates were replaced.

In the mid-1990s the saltwater lake was again afflicted with a toxic bloom of blue-green algae. As it could be deadly to animals (although not birds or fish) and might also cause people to develop eye irritation, fever, rashes, vomiting, diarrhoea, and pain in muscles and joints, visitors were warned to keep their pets away from the water and to avoid contact with it themselves. Boating and boardsailing were suspended.

The glutinous mud-brown globular clumps of algae thrived in the bright sunlight and warm waters of exceptionally hot weather, sinking to the bottom in the evening but resurfacing when the sunlight reappeared. Unfortunately this coincided with maximum use of the park by holidaymakers. Once autumnal rain and gloom arrived, it died but too late to rescue the seasonal boat-hire business. Perversely, these plants, usually found in freshwater, had only affected the saltwater boating lake and not the smaller lakes inhabited by the ducks and geese.

For three consecutive years the toxic algal mats plagued the lake. Reopened for boating over the Easter Bank Holiday weekend of 1997, after tests revealed the algae had disappeared, it had to be closed again after just four days when a different strain emerged. On Monday 28 July a frustrated Geoff Tapper removed his sixty boats from the lake and put them into storage after it was decided that there was no chance of clearing the toxic algae that summer.

Several disparate (if not desperate) solutions were suggested to combat and conquer the toxic blue-green algae: dumping decomposed straw into the lake; draining and dredging; and opening the sluice gates to allow tidal flushing. The Japanese electronics giant

One of the two nascent filter beds.

Barely credible … but it really happened. (*Bournemouth Daily Echo*)

Hitachi claimed it could coat the phytoplankton with a secret formula of ferromagnetic particles, then scoop the coagulated viscous mess up with magnets. Scientists at Reading University suggested that a special type of seaweed could do the trick. Researchers in Perth, Australia, recommended a chemically modified clay (not readily obtainable in the south of England).

In 2000, however, the Environment Agency carried out further tests and told the Borough of Poole that they had no conclusive answer. More tests, extra monitoring over months, and perhaps a package of measures would be needed to suppress the algal blooms. The algae might in any case be a nationwide problem. In 2003 it made an unwelcome return to Poole Park, forcing closure of the boating lake for the first time since the four successive closures in the late 1990s (see Boating).

DREDGING

In 2007 the lake was dredged. The prohibitive cost of removing the spoil in road vehicles was avoided by using it to create a cluster of five islets which, in a few years will establish themselves with vegetation and provide extra refuges for water fowl. Critics point out that the extra depth gained was a mere 20cm (barely 8in), and that 10cm (4in) was then lost when the level of the lake had to be lowered so as not to overwhelm the low-lying new islets, and the lake was deep enough anyway for the boats now used by Rockley Watersports. More eco-concerned voices argue that a layer of decomposed detritus had accumulated over decades on the lake bed, with potential for pollution and possible disease, the removal of which was justification in itself for the effort and outlay incurred.

Two additional reed beds were strategically located to the north east of the lakeside, where it is hoped they will act as filters to run off water from the land that might otherwise deposit oil or other pollution in the lake.

OIL SPILLAGE

On Friday evening, 2 June 1995 at 8 p.m. a fast-response team from the National Rivers Authority rushed to the park where 50 gallons of stinking oil had spilled – later investigation revealed – from an underground culvert in the North Road area behind Poole College into the lake. As there were at least 300 connections to the system, it was impossible to determine if it had been dumped from a domestic or commercial source, otherwise a prosecution that resulted in a conviction would have rendered those responsible liable for a fine of up to £20,000. A threat to water and wildlife alike, fortunately the wind direction had not spread the concentrated 20m by 5m spill and come 3 a.m. on Saturday morning the team had booms in place to contain it and sludge-gulping pumps to suck the oil slick from the surface of the water.

OOPS!

Because the parking areas adjacent to the boating lake lack a raised edge, now and again a car topples into the lake, either through driver error or when deliberately abandoned and dumped by a joy rider. Whether by chance or crime, it happens. In 1983 a V-registration hatchback swerved into the model-yacht lagoon after colliding with one of the brick-built pillars at the Whitecliff Gate. In October 1991 a stolen Ford Cortina was abandoned with the front two-thirds in the saltwater lake. A few years later a Ford Escort ended up with all four wheels on the bottom a few yards out from the side of the lake.

In November 1994 a saloon by the model-boat enclosure lived up to its name when a Volvo (which means 'I roll' in Latin) nosedived into the water after the elderly male driver got out. A female passenger emerged shaken and wet but unhurt. The fire brigade winched the car back onto dry land, and the couple drove away.

On Friday 3 November 2000, at about 2 p.m., a twenty-nine-year-old man was taken to hospital for a check up, then released, after the car he was driving somehow put its nearside wheels over the edge and tipped sideways into the lake. The maroon Peugeot 205 was later winched out of the water suffering from damage consistent with partial immersion.

THE SLUICES

Opening the sluice gates to flush the lake periodically and so freshen it, minimises the swarms of midges that otherwise breed there. Similarly the depth can be reduced for maintenance work around the perimeter of the lake by opening the gates and simply waiting for low tide to expose the surrounding foreshore. This is best done during one of the predictable spring ebb tides which are lower than the weaker intervening neap tides.

The sluice channel can be a hazard. Many years ago, when the lake was having one of its two or three annual refills, a sailing dinghy in Parkstone Bay was caught and capsized by the strong inflow of current and its occupant drowned.

It is also a lure to dogs. On Thursday 8 August 1996 a golden retriever was drowned there. One of several shocked eye-witnesses walking their own dogs was a Poole councillor. In July 2003, another golden retriever, exploring a gap in the fence by the tidal sluices, fell into the water. The dog's owner and a second woman who went to help her both lost their footing on the concrete sides and toppled in themselves. All three were swept into the gates and pinned there by the force of the flushing water. Two men reached the women and the dog within minutes, dragging them back onto dry land. The trio escaped with only cuts, bruises and shock, but the incident led to renewed calls for improved safety to the gates. A floating boom now prevents anyone or anything approaching it from the lake, and notices exist on the lakeside path warning of danger.

In 2004 five reed beds were installed at both ends of the sluice channel as an experiment in filtration; but, while the reeds did not flourish, they did unfortunately collect litter.

SPORT AND RECREATION

What I know most surely about morality and the duty of man I owe to sport.
Albert Camus, French writer and Nobel Prize winner, 1913–1960

BOWLS

In 1929 the putting green was begun and the following year two bowling greens of Cumberland turf were opened. Here Poole Park Bowling Club achieved national fame in the 1930s by winning the Pairs Championships of the English Bowling Association twice in successive years, and Mr E.P. Baker became the Singles Champion of England in 1932, 1946, 1952 and 1955. The club's greens were also good enough for the final rounds of the National Triples Championship in 1958 and 1959.

Until the year 2001 members endured two separate pavilions which dated from the 1930s (for gentlemen) and 1950s (for ladies), both of which were inadequate if all of the members entitled to use them turned up at the same time. In January 2000 Poole's planning chiefs approved the demolition of these two dilapidated structures, one wooden the other brick-built, and their replacement by the present £240,000 stylish building. Fit for the conservation area in which it is located, the single-story pavilion can accommodate all 117 male and fifty-three female members who use the two greens, with a club room, kitchen, store/ticket office, toilet and changing facilities. It was officially opened on Friday 22 June 2001 by the Deputy Mayor of Poole, Cllr Mrs Joyce Jones.

Bowling in the park, 1988 ... (Michael J. Allen Photography)

... and a serene corner of the putting green in 2007. (Geoffrey Budworth)

The entrance to the bowling club.

The bowling club's 2001 pavilion.

Turf and tape, when millimetres matter …

Humorous cartoon by Dorset-based artist and illustrator Danny Byrne.

CRICKET

In 1902 Poole Council agreed with Mr Manfield, secretary of Dorset County Cricket Club, to spend up to £300 on alterations to the ground within the park so that county matches could be played there. The cricket pavilion cost £260 to build in the early 1900s. The clock was added in 1960.

In 1953 successful business entrepreneur 'Ronnie' Cornwall, son of a Poole alderman and father of the renowned author John le Carré, brought together the RTA Cornwall XI. So many notable cricketers agreed to appear that each team consisted of twelve players. Among them were Sidney Barnes (Australia), Learie (later 'Sir Learie') Constantine and Roy Marshall (West Indies), J.M. Parks (Sussex) and D.N. Silk (Cambridge University), who would become president of the MCC. It was estimated that they drew in 8,000 spectators, who were greatly entertained by a one-day match in which 453 runs were scored. The opposing team Poole Park XII did well and claimed a moral victory after dismissing eight of the visitors for 259 runs, then going on to score 194 for the loss of only three wickets before stumps were drawn.

By the mid-1950s, the lack of maintenance during the war years was apparent. The drains of the cricket pitch had silted up and Dorset county match umpires declared the outfield unfit for play. In 1963, however, Dorset cricket club played two of their Minor Counties fixtures on the resuscitated cricket pitch and outfield.

In 1997 Wessex Water had proposed an underground tank at a cost of £600,000, to fill with dilute sewage during storms when the old and now inadequate sewers were full to overflowing. It would be 12.5m in diameter and 7–8m deep (½m of which would project above the ground). Opponents, outraged as usual, stated that 'a cess pit in a public park was unacceptable'.

The modest, but not unstylish, tiled building a couple of bowling lengths along from the pavilion unveiled by the mayor in September 1999 is the pumping station. The colourful mosaic was designed by youngsters from Baden-Powell and St Peter's Middle School. The displaced roof tiles result from other young people carelessly kicking their balls onto the roof.

CYCLING

The more or less circular cycle track enclosing the cricket pitch is not banked, and today might be mistaken for an unusually wide footpath, although youngsters on tricycles and small bikes seem to know instinctively what it is for. You might even meet a unicyclist pedalling his or her way around the ⅓-mile circuit.

Charles Lane used to lap this track at the turn of the century when training for the Weymouth Cycle Club. The rigid amateur rules prohibited prizes that were 'consumable' (from food, drink and money to items such as clothing that could be worn and worn out) which is why winnings had to be permanent mementos, such as dinner services, sets of cutlery and trophies in the shape of cups or shields. It was said that the top riders would arrive early to see what was on offer, and then agree with one another to swap any prizes won so that all had something they did not already own.

Steven Burge no doubt still did some training on this track. He was the English champion and a member of the long-established Poole Wheelers Club who had won the City of Bath Challenge Cup in 1895 and 1896 as well as numerous local and regional competitions. He was a bootmaker by trade and in the 1930s worked for J.A. Hawkes & Sons Ltd in Poole High Street.

In the early 1930s Bill Harvell led the Wheelers to victory here in the British Team Pursuit Championship and beat the English champion Len Southall.

FOOTBALL

One football match played in the park on 17 October 1908 was a second qualifying round tie in the English Cup between Longfleet St Mary's and Exeter City, in front of 4,000 people who each paid 6*d.* for entry. Longfleet belonged to the Dorset Football League while mighty Exeter, then of the South League, was the first professional team to play in Poole. The game ended in a one-one draw after seventeen-year-old inside-forward Tom Dempsey had put the home side ahead, and the goalkeeper Bert Andrews repeatedly saved the local team to keep the score level.

A week later the two sides met again at St James' Park, Exeter, in appalling weather conditions, when the home side won 10-0 (the worst defeat in the Poole side's history) despite sterling work yet again from Bert Andrews. He went on to play over 500 games for Longfleet St Mary's, missing only twelve, between 1898 and 1913.

FUN AND FROLICS

The completion of an electric tramway between Poole railway station and County Gates (the western boundary of Bournemouth), at a cost in excess of £64,000, which began to carry fare-paying passengers on Saturday 6 April 1901, was the cause of a celebratory civic tea party in the park given by the Mayor of Poole, Alderman G. Watkin accompanied by his town sergeant Mr Venables. A local caterer, Mr G.W. Green, provided tea for 200 guests, while D (Poole) Company of the 1st Volunteer Battalion of the Dorchester Regiment Band 'discoursed a nice selection of music'.

Throughout the 1920s and '30s, between the two world wars, there were funfairs, fancy-dress parades, country-dancing competitions and fireworks. More recently park users have watched everything from free-fall parachuting, to an 'It's a Knockout' competition and line dancing.

On Saturday and Sunday 25-26 May 1996, as part of an eco-conscious 'Green Week', a road show in the park featured every imaginable method of conserving Earth's finite resources, from electric cars to solar-powered fountains, as well as 'Croissant Neuf' (the world's only wind and solar-powered big-top circus).

In July 1997, when its planned raft race had to be abandoned due to a recurrence of toxic algae in the saltwater lake, the Poole Round Table held a 'wacky wheelbarrow race' instead.

Motor Sport

Noise within the park had been mostly limited to the irksome calls of peacocks, until, in 1936, the West Hants Light Car Club held speed trials there; but 5,000 or more spectators, including the townspeople, cheerfully endured the deafening decibels from highly tuned revving engines, the whine of superchargers, and the grinding of mistimed gear changes.

The following year the club had changed its name to the West Hants & Dorset Car Club, and the weather was perfect, although attendance was down slightly due to counter attractions. But the entry had grown. Charlie Martin received the Poole Trophy and a £50 cash prize from Mayor Mervyn J. Wheatley, for knocking split seconds off the record of George Hartwell who had to be content with the Poole Chamber of Trade Cup for being the fastest club member. Lord Austin was to drive the smallest car, a 744cc with a reputation for being fast, but unfortunately it suffered mechanical trouble and did not start.

In 1938 the entry was up again, to eighty-two, but the crowd had halved to 2,600. However absentees were able to listen to a report on the West Region wireless that evening by its motoring correspondent Dean Delamont, who would later become an official of the Royal Automobile Club. The biggest thrill of the day came when CI Craig's Bugatti went into a spectacular spin and only just missed the water fountain (in which club marshals were cooling their supplies of beer).

In July 1939 the skies were sombre and rain fell during the afternoon of the trial. This fourth (and last) meeting, in July 1939, began under sombre skies and falling rain, but was abandoned after Whitfield Semmence's car spun badly on the slippery surface and came to an abrupt stop. The Mayoress, wife of Mayor Joseph Bright (in the second of what would turned out to be his seven-year wartime term of office) presented the fastest driver trophy to I.F. Connell who had competed in a 4-litre Darracq, after which everyone went home to prepare for the Second World War.

After the war, the road surface was no longer adequate and the trials went to other venues. Such events would be hard to justify now. Even then they were astonishing. Some of the cars hit speeds in excess of 100mph, only a few yards from spectators who were protected by mere chestnut fencing and the few straw bales placed to protect corporation property. The drivers were daredevils in flannel bags (trousers) and plimsolls who did not wear crash helmets, although some sported linen helmets, goggles and overalls.

As recently as January 1988, however, up to 150 high-performance rally cars competed in the National Mazda Winter Rally around 1½-mile course from the Baiter and through Poole Park via the keyhole bridge.

Running

All kinds of athletic events have been staged in the park over the years where three laps of the cycle track were reckoned to be a mile. Percy Hodge, the Olympic steeplechase champion once ran in a Poole Mile Handicap and won easily (having given some of the entrants half-a-lap start).

The annual Poole Marathon was established in 1986 with a roughly circular course around the entire borough, starting and finishing within the park, that included a scenic sea-level circuit of the Sandbanks peninsula.

SPONSORED EVENTS

Some deem all sponsored events as little more than begging, the imaginary rattle of unauthorised collecting boxes made lawful by the appearance of some physical endeavour in exchange for alms. Nevertheless, it is now so familiar as a method of raising funds within the voluntary sector that it appears mean spirited to refuse a donor's signature for whoever is doing what.

In the autumn of 1980 a five-year-old boy dribbled a ball with a hockey stick around thirteen laps (4 miles) of the park's cycle track to raise cash for a renovation of the East Gate Lodge. In May 1991 over forty children (all under five years of age) tricycled, bicycled or scootered around the track for the National Childbirth Trust's antenatal teaching programme. And on Sunday 14 May 2006 a five-year-old girl ran non stop around a 5km course in a time of thirty-eight minutes and thirty seconds, beating hundreds of woman older than herself, in a 'Run for Life' event in aid of Cancer Research.

In January 1990, twenty-five Poole Sea Cadets embarked on a twenty-five-hour non-stop sail around the saltwater lake. Becalmed for five hours during the night, with sub-zero temperatures and ice forming on every surface, they were compelled to row so as to complete the challenge in aid of the new Delph Wood residential centre for the severely handicapped.

In 1992 five teams of four rowers each rowed from midday on Saturday to midday on Sunday, steering via fluorescent course markers during the hours of darkness, to raise cash for Poole Voluntary Beach Lifeguards. The twenty oarsmen and women totalled 340 miles, with two teams achieving seventy miles each.

That same year, starting at 6 p.m. on Friday 16 October, members of the Poole Amateur Rowing Club completed a twenty-four-hour marathon. Twenty-six male and eight females (age range ten to thirty-five), in coxed fours (coxswains extra) rowed in three- to four-hour spells around flashing buoys. The night was warm and boredom was combated with games of 'I-Spy'. The original total distance of 1,000 miles proved unattainable but a useful amount was raised for RNLI funds.

SUMMER FESTS

In 2004, 2005, 2006 and 2007 the Friends of Poole Park held a series of August Bank Holiday weekend Fests. These ambitious events featured art, craft, alternative therapy and trade stalls; demonstrations and free taster sessions by sports organisations; circus skills and other workshops; fun rides and slides; as well as live music venues and dancing. Held over two days, each event attracted tens of thousands of visitors who were invited to put cash donations in the buckets of roaming volunteers. The 2007 event received a generous £20,000 for the Friends of Poole Park to spend on improving the park's facilities, bringing the total gained by all four Fests to £62,000.

SWIMMING

Preceding the municipal elections in November 1908 the council resolved to provide a swimming bath on a site near the saltwater lake. John Elford the borough engineer later drew up plans but it would be fifteen years before they were implemented. The *Poole Guide* for 1929 reported:

Sam Budworth, the author's grandson, tackles the park's fourth Summer Fest (2007). (Geoffrey Budworth)

'An Open-Air Sea Water Swimming Bath is now under construction at Kingland Road, Seldown. The water will be continuously filtered and sterilised in the latest principles of hygiene.'

The resulting pool, surrounded by a high fence, was located at the south-west corner in Park Lake Road, overlooked by the railway and the gasworks. An uninviting rectangular tank, it looked like another one of the 'fill-and-empty' pools of the period, clean (but cold) on Mondays and warmed up a couple of degrees (but filthy) by the weekend, chlorinated and pH buffered by the rough-but-ready method known in the trade as 'bucket-and-chuck it'. Pupils

Early morning in 2008, the Park Lake Road houses (built in the 1930s). (Geoffrey Budworth)

at the adjacent Poole Grammar School and from Parkstone Grammar School for Girls (who from 1951–1955 were marched in classes to and from the pool) recall, however, a triple-layered fountain at the shallow end. That cascade was an aerator, believed then to add sparkle to the pool, confirming that it was indeed turned over, heated and treated by circulation and dosing pumps in a pool-water-treatment plant room.

This pool was still in occasional use until 1961, after which it was demolished and the land it occupied became a half-acre mini-wilderness. Until in the early 2000s an eco-village housing development arose and might have consumed it. The Friends of Poole Park moved quickly to confirm that plans drawn up in 1887 showed clearly that it was within the boundary of the park … when the builders backed off and left it untouched.

In 2008 the junior section of the Poole Harbour Canoe Club will locate changing accommodation and boat storage there.

TENNIS

Sportily attired Edwardian gents and ladies played tennis on an area of grass set aside for the game. Although women had, since the 1880s, taken an active part in an increasing range of sports, they continued to be hampered by cumbersome clothing, and some were content that way. In 1909 Mrs Sterry, on becoming British ladies' champion for the fifth time, declared, 'To my mind nothing looks smarter or more in keeping with the game than a nice clinging white skirt [about 2in off the ground], white blouse, white band, and a pale coloured silk tie and white collar'. Not to mention white stockings, shoes and a hat. Later the English writer (and Prime Minister's wife) Lady Cynthia Asquith recalled, '… even our lawn tennis dresses, usually like nursery maids wear, made of white piqué, were so long that it was impossible to take a step back without treading on them.' Trousers were not worn until the 1920s.

The existing tennis hard courts are a late-twentieth-century creation.

A rare view of the 1930s swimming pool. (Andrew Hawkes)

Tennis in the summer of 1923. (Author's collection)

SUNDRIES

How nice it is to know things.

Bertrand Russell, 3rd Earl, Nobel Prize winner, English philosopher,
mathematician and writer, 1872–1970

BANDSTANDS

Bandstands and boating lakes were Victorian innovations. The first one in a public park appeared in West Bromwich, Staffordshire in 1887, and as late as the 1950s bands were hired to play on summer weekends from the one in Poole Park.

COAT OF ARMS

The stone coat-of-arms on the side of the Seldown Gate Lodge features a mermaid (minus arms) atop a medieval helm, a shield with three sea shells and a dolphin, beneath which is a scroll with the Latin motto *Ad Morem Villae de Poole* (According to the Custom of the Town of Poole).

The first representation of a coat of arms resembling this was on an old seal from the late 1300s, predating the order of King Henry V in 1417 forbidding the bearing of arms without authority from the Crown. In 1563 Clarenceux King-of-Arms (an official from the College of Arms) visited Poole and confirmed this previously unauthorised coat of arms. The relevant document is preserved in the town's archives.

In 1976 the College of Arms granted the addition of 'supporters', a lion with a long sword or épée, plus a dragon with a silver oar to symbolise the courtesy title still held today by the mayor as 'Admiral of the Port of Poole'.

Naturalism tends to be viewed with disfavour in heraldry, but Poole's images of the mermaid and dolphin have both been modernized, in the latter's case to take account of the fact that it is a highly evolved and intelligent mammal.

Bandstand and bicyclist (both alas long gone) in 1922. (Author's collection)

COUNCIL CONCERNS

In 2005 a landmark decision was taken by the council to waive the usual charge on activities by community groups raising cash for charitable purposes. This followed an outcry after they quoted an administration charge of £26 for 'support and guidance' at a sponsored 'Toddlethon' (for under three-year-olds).

The following year park watchers grew concerned over the council decision to issue a general license to Poole Park (and other open spaces within the borough) for plays, dance, films, live music and sporting events until 11 p.m. Objections from residents, mostly to do with locations other than Poole Park, cited late-night noise and disturbance from amplified music, the increased risk of burglary, anti-social antics and fires (either deliberate or accidental). In fact the entertainments licence had in mind charities and other voluntary sector bodies who might wish to use the park but be put off by the administration costs and time delays in obtaining individual licences.

GUNS

Across the road from the East Lodge, parked on the grass, was a 125mm breech-loading German field gun that had been given to Poole as a trophy after the First World War. The gun remained in the park until 1928, when it was removed to the Poole ex-Servicemen's Club in North Road, and then in 1940 it was sold as scrap metal for the sum of £2 13s. 0d.

Another gun stood in an area of the park called 'the gravel patch' close by the original tea rooms. This was a Russian muzzle-loading cannon, adorned by an eagle, given to Poole after one or other of the two sieges of Sebastopol, a seaport in the Crimea of the south-west USSR. This piece of ordnance had originally stood outside the Guildhall, but was moved to the park, and subsequently to the Stert esplanade where it remained until the late 1930s (or early years of the Second World War) when it too was sold for scrap.

SHORELINE

It is evident that, prior to the park's creation, tidal waters reached the Sloop public house (aka the Conjuror's Half Crown), now on the far side of the gyratory one-way traffic system and beyond the civic offices (where the remains of jetty piles were unearthed during pre-1930 work on the foundations).

SQUIRRELS

Back in the 1940s red squirrels still bred and begged in Poole alongside the grey variety. Now the shyer reds survive only in isolated habitats (such as Brownsea Island and the Isle of Wight), while the intrusive greys scurry wild and free in the park. It remains to be seen whether or not they survive the recently reported proliferation of black squirrels with their aggressive intolerance of sharing territory.

TELEPHONE BOXES

Before the ownership of mobile phones, park users occasionally complained to the council that they had to return to the streets and buildings outside the park gates in order to make calls. So in May 1984 four classic K6 'Jubilee' red telephone boxes, originally introduced to commemorate the Silver Jubilee in 1935 of King George V, were installed (see Guided Walk). Once a familiar sight on British streets this model was designed by leading architect Sir Giles Gilbert (1880–1960) who won a Post Office competition with it. HM Prison inmates stripped, reglazed and repainted these cast-iron structures, each of which weighs ¾ton. Poole Borough Council owns the quartet, which tap into BT landlines.

This 125mm ex-First World War German field gun remained in the park until 1928. (Andrew Hawkes)

The muzzle-loading Russian cannon from Sebastopol was an attraction until around 1940. (Andrew Hawkes)

Two of the park's four K6 telephone kiosks flank a litter bin in the shape of a ship's mooring bollard (hinting at Poole's maritime history). (Geoffrey Budworth)

Dog Waste Bins

In 1991 the council installed perhaps the most expensive dog-waste bins in England. For the total cost of thirty-five fibreglass cast-iron finish receptacles, each emblazoned with the town's dolphin crest, was £12,500 – £357 each.

Information Kiosk

In 2007 – an upbeat year, what with dredging the lake, creating five islets, refurbishing and renaming Central Park Café (with its ice rink) – the disused ice-cream kiosk opposite the Rockley Watersports area was reallocated by the borough's Leisure Services Department to the Friends of Poole Park. The long and low Art Deco style building was renovated at a cost of over £8,000, with another £2,000 spent on storage equipment and furniture, to provide both a committee room and a visitors' information centre staffed by volunteers at weekends and in the summer holidays.

TRAFFIC

They paved paradise and put up a parking lot ...
                    Joni Mitchell, Canadian singer-songwriter

During its first decade the park was a place where nannies with prams could stroll along the empty roads and children whip tops, bowl hoops or play tag, with no thought of motor vehicles. Wheeled traffic consisted of horse-drawn carts and carriages.

A miniature 'Gemmar' ware tankard with a Czech maker's mark used between 1918 and 1945). (Salisbury Photo Imaging Ltd)

A bird's-eye view (*c.* 1980) of the freshwater and boating lakes, cricket field, cycle track, Swan Lake Café, miniature railway station, model motorboat enclosure and model yacht lagoon catwalk, as well as the rear gardens of Twemlow Avenue houses that adjoin the park. (Brian Merrifield)

But, by 1914 this idyll was trespassed upon by cars, motorcycles and the occasional sightseeing charabanc. The first public transport from the East Gate of Poole Park to the Haven at Sandbanks was a fleet Model T ('Tin Lizzie') Ford motorcars.

In March 1954 the council was advised that Poole Park miniature railway was liable to pay the local business rate of tax, and how this came about has a motoring link. For several years the corporation retained a local surveyor and estate agent named E. Harker Curtis to undertake property valuation work, and he owned a Sunbeam car which he drove everywhere at exactly 20mph – no faster but no slower. The speed limit within the park was then just 8mph, and Harker Curtis had been seen several times speeding. Despite verbal warnings he refused to slow down, so the park superintendent Ernie Gale instructed two of his most reliable keepers, Ernie Fisher and Tom Forsey (with his Alsation dog 'Bolus') to catch the offender in the act and report him. As Harker Curtis routinely drove through the park on his way home to lunch, the two men simply stood a measured quarter of a mile apart on the road and clocked him with a stopwatch. Whether or not, as some said later, this irked the offender into advising the corporation, wrongly, that their miniature railway was rateable; it took five years of costly legal appeals to establish that he had misled them (see Miniature Railway).

SPEED

The original speed limit was 8mph and park keepers would stop and verbally warn drivers who they estimated exceeded that limit. Half-a-century later, to combat speeding, the council invoked this old byelaw; and, although no prosecutions were brought for speeds under 15mph, there were twenty-one prosecutions in February 1953 and forty-two the following month. A council committee discussed prohibiting traffic altogether, but decided that would cause parking problems elsewhere, and maybe prevent some people from visiting the park at all. In 1990, for the park's centenary celebrations, the roads were closed to traffic (initially for a week) but were reopened after just three days when visits dropped noticeably.

The committee even flirted with the notion of reclaiming an area on the eastern side of the 60-acre boating lake for car parking, but ultimately rejected it in the face of opposition from park users.

Crossing the traffic streaming in both directions along Parkstone Road was a risky venture for anyone – but noticeably elderly people and anyone with children – until, in 1996, the popular singer/comedian Max Bygraves opened a pelican crossing by the Memorial Gate. This was a unique street provision funded largely by donations: £4,000 from the council and a substantial £11,000 from Methodist Homes for the Aged.

Concerned to safeguard whatever could be preserved of the park's traditional appeal, the Friends of Poole Park and the council agreed that the fewest possible signs and road markings should be installed. Any factors which impeded traffic – from unhurried geese and swans wandering over the carriageway to asphalt corrugations caused by tree roots – were tolerated as means to slowing car speeds. In 1994 new speed-restriction humps were installed on the park's roads. Combined with pinch-points where the carriageway narrows to a single alternate lane of traffic flow, these are as high as the footway kerbs, not only slowing car speeds but providing platforms for pedestrians (especially those who are less mobile) to traverse the roadway without the need for pedestrian-crossing markings. Of course motorists objected at the outset, as did organisers of the annual Poole Marathon who described them as 'diabolical'.

In 2005 the chairman of the Friends of Poole Park reported to the Dorset Police that speeds of over 50mph had been registered in the park, despite the permitted 20mph limit, and asked if this might be monitored at peak times (5–7 p.m.) at least once a year. Police responded that

The back-bending labour of bedding plants. (Geoffrey Budworth)

current traffic calming measures deployed within the park were considered effective but it had sent a request for the Beat Team to make 'a visual appearance' (Where do they learn such language?) in the park whenever possible in order to deter speeding.

PARKING

Hoping to deter motorists from leaving their vehicles in the park all day, the borough council introduced a one-hour time limit along one side of Kingland Road and in the two car parks. This irked both those who had been successfully avoiding town-centre car-parking charges while at work and genuine park visitors who pointed out that sixty minutes was too short a period to take a walk, feed the ducks, play with the children or grandchildren, and enjoy a snack or a meal in the café/restaurant. The arbitrary limit had to be modified. There are now four car parks and several short roadside sections where, subject to generous time limits, parking is permitted either free of charge or by pay-and-display.

TREES, SHRUBS AND PLANTS

Now, nature, as I am only too well aware has her enthusiasts, but on the whole, I am not to be counted among them. To put it rather bluntly, I am not the type who wants to go back to the land; I am the type who wants to go back to the hotel.

'Fran' Lebowitz, American author

For a century the corporation relied for its supply of plants on the nursery garden in Kingland Road which yearly produced a million plants, half of them to be planted within the borough.

Some of the surplus went to other local authorities, and the remainder was sold to green-fingered local residents by a friendly staff dispensing not only produce but expert advice too. This long relationship was lost in 1998, however, when the nursery's management was outbid and the contract reassigned. As none of the applicants had opted to retain the site, it closed at the end of the year, leaving residents who had campaigned to save it disappointed and saddened by its loss.

Chestnut Nursery

The 2.2-acre site remains part of Poole Park, the covenant dated 3 March 1886 between Lord Wimborne and the Corporation of Poole restricting it to park use, but not for car parking or building. In October 2001 the site was taken over by SWOP (the Sheltered Work Opportunities Project) to be operated as Chestnut Nursery. The five greenhouses were repaired by volunteers, the site cleared, and the enterprise now opens to the public six days a week selling a wide variety of perennials, shrubs, ornamental grasses and seasonal crops.

The incoming contractor Simon Wreford was – at the age of just twenty-nine – perhaps England's youngest established landscape gardener, and his dynamic company Wreford Landscapes Ltd, was more than up to the job of soft landscaping in Poole Park. Their supply of high-quality shrubs and semi-mature trees were obtained from leading nurseries in mainland Europe with whom they had long-term relationships. Their mobile work squads, whether toing and froing aboard battery-operated John Deere runabouts or backs bent over bedding plants, blended a range of sow, mow and grow skills with the latest health-and-safety and COSHH (Control of Substances Hazardous to Health Regulations 1999) practices now required to work in public areas. Site-specific activities were overseen and monitored with the kind of management team calculated to reassure the borough's contract managers that projects would be completed on time and within budget.

Shrubs and Plants

Hundreds of shrubs are replaced in the park every year. This can involve the removal of all existing plants in late August/early September; then killing regrowth of perennial weeds and bindweed in September; compost during the winter months; and replanting in March (having left time for any remaining toxins in the ground disperse). Notable Dorset plants within the park include bog pimpernel (*Anagallistenella*), bitter vetch (*Lathyrus linifolius*) and hard grass (*Parapholis strigosa*). Another nationally rare one is spiral tasselweed (*Ruppia cirrhosa*).

Surprisingly, such a benign activity as gardening can engage and enrage park users, as well as their elected local politicos. In 1981 the decision to plant new shrubbery and erect a protective fence around the freshwater lake (see Miniature Railway) so incensed one councillor, because the additions would block sightlines and access to the waterside and its wildlife, that he staged a walk out from the committee room, protesting that he would never again attend a meeting presided over by that mayor.

Trees

Trees were well established within the park before the First World War. Massed or as isolated individuals, they make pleasing scenery as well as providing a habitat for wildlife and many other organisms, while their large size and relatively long lives adds perspective to humankind's existence. They also prevent erosion, recycle water, oxygen and carbon dioxide, and reflect the rotation of the seasons.

The immature chestnut tree avenue leading into the park from the East Gate (above), and a section of surviving trees in 2007 (below).

Above and below: Trees near the Swan Lake Café uprooted by the 1987 hurricane. Some are blocking the miniature railway track. (Brian Merrifield)

The 'umbrella' tree adjacent to the Copse Close playing field. (Geoffrey Budworth)

The park has approximately 1,100 trees, some of which owe their existence to 'Plant a Tree Year' in 1972/73 when private planting was encouraged. Since 2000 an estimated 112 have been installed. Many located by the edge of the park are now protected by Tree Preservation Orders and tawny owls roost in some of the horse chestnut and fir trees.

The broad aim of tree management within the park is to create and maintain a population of various ages and maturity, except for the formal avenue of horse chestnuts leading from the East Gate, and time-honoured features such as the pines near the restaurant. From time to time unplanned planting may become necessary, such as after the 1987 hurricane that devastated the UK and uprooted as many as two dozen prime trees, mostly pine, around the exposed areas of the Swan Lake Café and the Whitecliff Gate.

As old trees die or become unsafe they are replaced. Regrettably, over time, this has resulted in nearly half of the avenue of chestnut trees being removed. Only fifteen survive. The decision to fell others will be unavoidable sooner rather than later; and, so as to avoid an unsightly mix of old and young trees, all of the remainder should perhaps be removed and replaced at once. Horse chestnut trees were a Victorian vogue and, while an adult with childhood memories may wish to see like replaced with like, English Heritage has recommended that the choice should be some other suitable deciduous species.

The avenue of chestnut trees along Park Road from the Middle Park Gates to the Park Gates East was a fruitful source of conkers for generations of young boys, who either climbed the trees to hand pick them, or threw large bits of wood up into the branches to knock some down. Both activities invited the wrath of Mr Palmer, the head park keeper, who preferred them to let nature take its course and wait until the nuts fell of their own accord. This was too much to expect of boys seeking immediate rewards, who were prepared to risk one of his severe reprimands (and the threat of fetching a policeman).

The soils are deep sands and gravel with occasional bands of clay, of fairly low fertility, but capable of supporting a wide range of tree species (although it may be unsuitable for some). The major factor limiting plant growth is its exposure to salt-laden winds from the sea. The combination of the boating lake and Poole harbour beyond can have a detrimental effect on the height and vigour of trees in various parts of the park.

In 1990 the Borough of Poole commissioned a tree survey from an independent arboriculture consultant and this identified 1,076 trees comprising seventy-six varieties of broadleaves totalling 877 individuals (81.5 per cent of the total) and seventeen species of conifer totalling 199 individuals (the remaining 18.5 per cent). Knowledgeable tree spotters may identify: alders; beech, birch and black tupelo; cedars, chestnuts and cypress; elms; golden rain; hornbeam; Indian bean; Judas; katsura, Kentucky coffee; magnolia, maple and monkey puzzles; oaks; palms and poplars; redwoods, shagbark hickory; weeping willows, witch hazel and no doubt many more.

The current trend for less planting is a response to the number of trees that are now growing in the park, and the need to preserve its open character, although, because the park lies within a Conservation Area a tree must be planted to replace each one removed.

Wreford Landscapes Ltd declared itself immensely proud of what had been achieved when, in December 2007, that company's contract ended. The incoming organisation was the award-winning Continental Landscapes Ltd. Formed in 1989 this company is a member of the Dutch-based Krinkels Holding BV which operates in six Western Europe countries including the UK, with twenty-nine offices nationwide and a comprehensive fleet of vehicles and equipment. They employ over 800 people (including more than 100 professional management and supervisory staff), with a ground-staff team containing highly trained and experienced green keepers, arbiculturists and gardeners.

War Memorials

What price Glory?
                    Maxwell Anderson, American historical dramatist, 1888–1959

The First World War Cross
Not until 14 February 1927, after many meetings (some acrimonious), did Poole Council achieve a consensus to the erection of a war memorial for the men and women of the town who had been killed in the First World War. This was not due to any disregard for the sacrifice of individuals and the loss by their families. Previous mayors had done their very best to represent the wishes of the electorate, but those wishes were so diverse and contradictory, and their various advocates so uncompromising, that Guildhall debates had always ended unresolved. Eventually all agreed to erect something beautiful and relatively inexpensive on a suitable site, while those who had argued for 'something more practical' were asked to make their donations to the hospital although, in fact, very few did so.

The memorial was located within Poole Park, on the north side of the saltwater lake, remote from the noise of traffic on the A350 Parkstone Road (busy even then), approached via the Memorial Gate and a wide straight path through a small formal garden.

An impressive unveiling ceremony began at 3 p.m. on Sunday 16 October 1927, at 3 p.m., led by the Mayor Alderman Herbert Spencer Carter, in the company of his Sheriff Cllr R.H. Stokes and members of the council all in their robes of office. It was witnessed by an estimated 10,000 people, including: ex-servicemen and women of the British Legion

(Poole and Hamworthy); women of the Voluntary Aid Detachment (who nursed at home, abroad and in hospitals in action); the 179th Battery, Dorset Heavy Brigade, Royal Artillery; the 4th Dorset Regiment (Poole platoon); and the 14th Dorset Regiment (Poole territorials). Others assembled were the Boy Scouts, the Girl Guides, Poole fire brigade, the lifeboat crew, the St John Ambulance Brigade, members of the Harbour Board (Board of Guardians), and borough officials. The fund-raising War Memorial Committee with their energetic secretary W. Holden (deputy clerk) and subscribers were also present.

Under a cloudless sky 'to a crowd radiating genial warmth' General Lowe spoke for about five minutes on behalf of the ex-servicemen and women. A short service followed, in which the rector was assisted by non-conformist parsons. Three massed bands, the Poole Town Band, the Branksome Prize Band and the Gasworks Band, led hymn singing by the combined choirs of St James' and St Peter's Churches. The mayor then laid the first of more than 100 wreaths before making a short speech and pulling the unveiling cord.

The memorial was revealed to be a tall and slender cross of Purbeck stone, with narrow buttresses and brick shafts. Near the top were conventionally treated escallop shells and dolphins, a reference to the borough's coat of arms. The bricks were specially made from local clay, to give an impression of old walls, and were hard enough to permit their use in the steps and circular paving that surrounded the cross.

The design by J.S. Allner was in a fifteenth-century English architectural style, reminiscent of the naval era in which the town played no small part. On one side of the monument's base are the dates 1914–1918 and the weathered words 'They died that we would live'. On the other side has been added 1939–1945, 'We will remember them'. No individual names are inscribed upon it, which, some claim, renders it a timeless symbol to all from the town who had suffered and died on land and sea, and in the air, for freedom and in defence of their country in any conflict. After all, Poole men had fought at Crécy (1346) and Agincourt (1415), against the Spanish Armada (1588), and in the Crimean War (1853–1856).

On Wednesday 19 October at 3.58 p.m., three days after the unveiling, HRH the Prince of Wales (popular heir to the throne he would ultimately renounce) took time from a hectic programme of engagements in Bournemouth to lay a wreath at the new memorial during a short ceremony. He arrived in a Rolls-Royce car with Mayor Carter to much cheering and waving from a large crowd that included most of the borough's schoolchildren, admired the memorial, said he had never seen one like it, and asked who designed it. Walking among the assembled onlookers, the Prince displayed some impatience with officials and police who tried to keep them from pressing forward, and he paid special attention to the disabled ex-servicemen. 'Who's he?' he asked Alderman Carter as a distinguished general came forward, dismissing the senior officer with a curt handshake before turning away to chat with a man in a bath chair.

The Mountbatten Memorial

Earl Louis Mountbatten of Burma (1900–1979), KG, PC, GCB, OM, GCSI, GCIE, GCVO, DSO, who died on holiday at the age of seventy-nine when he was deliberately targeted and killed by an IRA bomb, had been the epitome of an English naval commander in the Second World War. Then, from 1943 until 1945 he was Supreme Allied Commander, South-East Asia, waging war on the Japanese in Hong Kong, China, Malaya and Sumatra. So it was that in peacetime he was appointed patron of the Burma Star Association, founded in the 1950s to represent the so-called 'Forgotten Army' of veterans whom he had led for three years of jungle warfare, and whose service had secured the true end of the Second World War on VJ (Victory in Japan) Day.

Left and above: The war memorial in 1927 …
and one of the Memorial Gate pillars.

Above: The war memorial with the
Mountbatten memorial cenotaph
and garden added in 1980. (Geoffrey
Budworth)

Right: The Mountbatten memorial.
(Geoffrey Budworth)

In the spring of 1980 a memorial rose bed to the men who died in the Burma campaign and those who have since suffered from their injuries, both physical and mental, was dedicated with the unveiling of a memorial cenotaph by Lt-Col. G.R.A. Brooking, vice-chairman of the UK Burma Star Association, on behalf of the Dorset branch of the Burma Star Association. It was attended by nearly seventy ex-servicemen, joined by sympathetic onlookers, a few of whom were living in the Far East when the Japanese invaded.

As many as 100 rose bushes were planted in this garden, one strain fittingly named 'Mountbatten' and the other 'Lord Louis'. In their midst a 5ft-high Purbeck-stone monument to him was unveiled by his daughter Lady Pamela Hicks. After the Last Post bugle call, a two-minute silence was observed, then reveille sounded. Lady Hicks spoke with deep appreciation of her father's respect for his 'Burma boys' and his enjoyment of their reunions. He wore his Burma Star with pride, she said, on every possible occasion. The memorial was inscribed 'In memory of those who died in the fighting in Burma (1941–1945)' together with the words of the Kohima Epitaph that is synonymous with Burma Star memorials wherever they are located:

> When you go home,
> Tell them of us and say,
> For your tomorrow,
> We gave our today.

Words attributed to John Maxwell Edwards, English classicist 1875–1958

WARTIME

There is nothing that war has ever achieved that we could not better achieve without it.
Henry Havelock Ellis, English physician and writer, 1859–1939

THE FIRST WORLD WAR (1914–1918)

During the First World War a local newspaper reported that wounded soldiers in bath chairs raced down the slope from Norton's Gate entrance … and troops marched through the park.

In the summer of 1919 Poole celebrated the end of hostilities with a number of events on Saturday and Sunday 26 and 27 July that year featuring 6,000 children aged between five and fifteen from local schools taking part in sports. The occasion was somewhat marred when a party from St Paul's School, with their teacher, Mr Stevens, entered the park via its Seldown Gate. As he helped the children down from the wagon, the horse moved forward suddenly, pitching several of the little ones head first onto the road. Three of them were 'quite seriously injured' but later made a full recovery. Just after noon on Saturday, ex-servicemen and the elderly poor were given a cold lunch in the park, followed by the spectacle of a civic procession.

THE SECOND WORLD WAR (1939–1945)

At the onset of the Second World War a mammoth recruiting parade was held within the park. Over 5,000 people turned up to see presentations by all those auxiliary organisations who would be involved in wartime activities at home, including: the Civil Defence; nursing; the Women's Voluntary Service (WVS); police, fire and ambulance. There was a military band from

Bovington; a fly past by the RAF; and, in the evening, a searchlight display. Controversially most of the newly enlisted Air Raid Precaution (ARP) Wardens refused to attend in protest at not having been allotted Warden Posts.

Later the Army dug five pits for anti-aircraft guns.

The Ministry of Supply persuaded the nation's housewives to surrender their aluminium pots and pans to be melted down as part of the war effort. In 1942, it turned its attention to scrap iron and took all of the railings from around the park for its furnaces. Ostensibly all of this raw material would be recycled to manufacture aeroplanes, tanks, guns and ammunition, but with 20/20 hindsight, it now appears to have been a well-intentioned initiative from Whitehall that failed to deliver any useful outcome.

During the night of 11/12 March 1941 a bomb damaged the open-air swimming pool near the railway line within the park but failed to explode. It was later detonated where it fell.

Throughout the Second World War, Poole harbour was Britain's sole international airport, with twice-weekly flying-boat services to Australia, India and North America. The Short Sunderlands of the British Overseas Airways Corporation, previously Imperial Airways (BOAC) – their noisy takeoffs and landings heard and seen in the park – carried not only essential mail but also VIPs who included King George VI, Winston Churchill and General de Gaulle, as well as ambassadors, diplomats, high-ranking service personnel, spies and celebrities of stage and screen.

Sometime in the mid-1940s a German raider dropped a bomb which demolished the rustic bridge across the narrow neck of the freshwater lake and killed two ducks. The incident was witnessed by members of the 4th Parkstone Sea Scouts who were out sailing in their three dinghies – *Cobweb*, *Tricolour* and *Fluffy Girl*. The traitorous British passport holder William Joyce, who was actually Brooklyn-born to Irish parents (nicknamed 'Lord Haw-Haw' because of his drawling speech), broadcast on Hamburg Radio a few days later that the Luftwaffe had inflicted serious damage to installations around Poole harbour.

In May 1944 the US Navy arrived in Poole harbour with sixty coastguard cutters, each 83ft long, destined for the D-Day Normandy beach landings. As the bulk petrol supply for these craft was considered too dangerous to be stored on the quayside, a large fuel-storage tank was built in the park near to the putting green at Middle Gate. A pipeline was then laid through the park, under the railway and into the Baiter, and from there to the quay for refuelling.

By the autumn of that same year Poole Council was winding down its war effort – although the war itself did not end until 1945 – and vegetable allotment holders in both Parkstone and Poole Parks (on what had been the tennis courts) were issued with notices to quit, but it was some time before the tennis courts could be relaid.

The VE (Victory in Europe) Day celebrations were as carefree and cheerful as anywhere in the land and the following day the armed forces held a victory parade through the park. This was followed later by many of the numerous auxiliary services who had also done wartime duties closer to home, including the ambulance staff; first-aid parties; Home Guard (dad's army); hospital staffs; National Fire Service; police (regular and special); rescue services; wardens; and Women's Voluntary Services (WVS).

On Monday 11 November 1946 a parade was held in front of the cricket pavilion to grant the Freedom of Poole to the Dorset Regiment.

Then, in an optimistic look ahead to normality, the park was the venue for an exhibition in June 1948 by fifty-six local firms displaying their produces and advising on skills required for work in their factories. Called 'Poole Can Make It', this was part of a post-Second World War enterprise to connect corporation and industry.

WILDFOWL

All the world seems in tune on a spring afternoon
When we're poisoning pigeons in the park.
Tom Lehrer, American singer-songwriter and satirist

Before the 1950s the only wildfowl in the park lakes were some mute swans, muscovy ducks, coot and moorhens. The first Canada geese were added to the freshwater lake in 1957 by the Dorset Wildfowlers. Other birds introduced later included mallards, sheldrakes, pochards, rosybills, and shovellers with some mute (and some black) swans, but it was the Canada geese who multiplied most. They nest and breed on Brownsea Island but fly daily to the park to graze the grass that is their staple diet; after which, having breakfasted early, they spend the rest of the day consuming whatever else human visitors give or leave for them.

Despite notices asking visitors not to feed the geese, many do. Anna Beiner from Wimbourne frequented the water's edge and fed the birds for many years in all weathers; and, when she died aged ninety-four, she left what small savings she had to continue feeding them. In recognition of this selfless devotion, her friend Ria Sanders persuaded the Poole Borough Open Spaces manager to permit the installation of a modest memorial, which was created by local stonemason Anthony Ives and the Bournemouth Engraving & Trophy Centre.

The quantity of goose droppings is now pestilential. A single bird can eat more grass each day than a sheep, and excrete the waste from its digestion every five minutes. That is around 100 sizeable cylindrical dumps per day amounting to 1kg (or 2lb) of goose poo; and, during peak times for park visitors, as many as 400 of these birds may daily produce an estimated 40,000 poops or one third of a ton of excreta. Anywhere the geese roam, it is impossible not to tread in something, while some grassy areas are impossible places to picnic. Fortunately only a rare few individuals and car windscreens receive a hit by dejecta from a flying goose, when the splay – as experts term it – is copious, sticky, mostly green, and smelling (victims report) like spinach soup.

Those who understood them say that the breeding success of these big, handsome and companionable birds, with their black heads, white chins and amiable 'ker-hunk' talk, is due to their sociable colonies and dutiful parenting skills. A gosling is rarely abandoned, or allowed to stray until it becomes lost or is picked off by a predatory seagull or cat.

Since the 1980s culling the geese has been discussed – and in 1990 the town clerk had to deny that the latest talk of a cull had anything to do with the prospective centenary celebration visit to the park by Prince Edward – but even those who want to limit geese numbers will not agree to direct (or indirect) killing. Few alternatives exist, although two celebrities, the late Linda McCartney and television sitcom writer Carla Lane, both offered to adopt the birds and relocate them on their own private estates.

When in July 1991 the nest of a Canada goose, with an egg in it, was found within the park itself, yet another proposal was put forward for reducing the geese numbers – a saucepan. The Royal Society for the Protection of Birds stated that the birds were put off breeding if hard-boiled eggs (or wooden dummies) were placed in their nests (although this assertion is contrary to the practice once customary in parts of rural England for poultry farmers to put a pottery egg inside hens' nests to encourage them to lay more).

When the subject of culling was resurrected in 2001, the council was persuaded once again that it would be unpopular, and could render them liable to prosecution under their own byelaws. Letting nature take its course through loss of eggs and small goslings had been ineffective.

Above and below: Canada geese breakfast in 2007 … then go on to elevenses. (Geoffrey Budworth)

Ria Sanders (admirer of the late Anna Beiner) and Matti Raudsepp (Open Spaces Manager), in August 2002, seek the approval of a Canada goose on the newly-installed 'Gooselady' plaque. (*Bournemouth Daily Echo*)

IN MEMORY OF
ANNA BEINER.
FONDLY KNOWN AS THE
'GOOSELADY'
1907 – 2002
WHO LOVED HER
FEATHERED FRIENDS OF
POOLE PARK FOR MANY YEARS

The 'Gooselady' plaque in 2007. (Geoffrey Budworth)

Pricking eggs at breeding sites might work. While, despite the impression given by Dickensian tales of Christmas feasts, a goose is a somewhat tough and unpalatable dish.

The long-standing debate about how to solve the problem of the goose droppings ended in action when the council bought an £8,600 'Goosebuster' machine. The Flowplant Harben DTM Water Jetting Unit is towed by a small van or lorry and pumps a water jet of 3,000lb/sq. in through a spinning nozzle, to blast droppings off pathways adjacent to the lakes. The diluted water flowing into the lake is thought not to provide food for algae or noticeably to affect the water quality. Unfortunately this mechanised poo-remover is ineffective on grass.

For a few days in the summer of 2004 a man patrolled with a bird of prey tethered to his wrist. The bird was encouraged to flap its wings at geese and goslings, driving them onto the water, but local park users complained to the Swan Rescue Sanctuary at Wimborne and a visiting wildlife officer confirmed that the raptor was a cause of distress for all of the water birds indiscriminately.

In 2006 a hand-held loud hailer became the latest weapon to be adopted by park rangers and Friends of the Park in the battle with the Canada geese. It broadcasts a recorded 'kronk' goose alarm call. The technique, copied from airport authorities, sends the large birds lumbering into the air or scrambling across grass and asphalt into one or other of the lakes where they settle apparently none the worse for the disturbance. Ducks and swans seem unaffected by the harsh sound.

Zoo

The sort of man who likes to spend his time watching a cage of monkeys chase one another, or a lizard catch flies, or a lion gnaw its tail, is precisely the sort of man whose mental weakness should be combated at the public expense and not fostered.
H.L. Mencken, American journalist and writer, 1880–1956

A zoo, designed and constructed to operate only during the summer opened in Poole Park on Saturday 1 June 1963, with a collection of some 120 exotic birds and mammals from many parts of the world. These included Greek tortoises, Vietnamese pot-bellied pigs, a Malabar squirrel, South African dwarf goats, and a Himalayan black bear called Chico. Birds ranged from budgerigars to buzzards and penguins.

A central petting enclosure for children contained golden hamsters, white rats, lambs, rabbits, guinea pigs and two very tame goats named Mary and Mabel.

The hardier species remained from Easter until the end of September, while more delicate tropical creatures able to cope only with the warmest months were swapped from time to time, and in winter all of the animals returned to their cold-weather sanctuary at Exmouth Zoo in Devon.

In 1971 the zoo's caging was approved by the Zoological Federation of Great Britain and the following year the zoo was taken over by Brian Pettit of West Moors (with his father as joint owner), and by the late 1970s Poole Park Zoo was attracting between 80,000 and 100,000 visitors a year.

But there was antagonism too, from a vocal minority opposed to wild animals in cages. The zoo was too small, they asserted, to make a worthwhile contribution to conservation, research or education. The animals and birds begged for food to relieve boredom and grew fat from inactivity. Anyway, all zoos depleted creatures in the wild by requiring a constant supply of rare species for captivity.

The RSPCA cited cramped cages, inadequate facilities, unsocial groupings, and the likelihood of mental suffering, adding that safety barriers were unsatisfactory and in their opinion the zoo should be closed before an animal escaped and attacked someone.

In November 1978, however, an independent veterinary report affirmed, '... most impressed with the proper and caring attitude ... and its good state of repair.' And the council stressed that there had never been an accident, while to reduce the operation to a mere children's park would not be viable; and by September 1980, as part of central government's Youth Opportunities Programme run by the Manpower Services Commission, the site was employing teenagers.

Co-owner Brian Pettit, who had been born in Kenya and grown up knowing wild and exotic animals in their natural habitats, said the complaints were unfounded and exaggerated by anti-zoo fanatics. Virtually all of the animals had been born captive and could not be returned to the wild. The bears and big cats could only be sold to be killed for their skins. In any case, he said:

> I don't see much future for animals in the wild because there is less and less of it every day ... the answer for the long term is captive breeding in zoos and safari parks ... If I had my way I would not open this place to the public ... open the doors to make revenue to pay for the upkeep of the animals.

Furthermore, he temporised, nobody knew how zoos might have to be altered pending implementation of the Zoo Licensing Act of 1981 which required the zoo to be approved by a zoo inspectorate before it could be granted a licence to open to the public. At a subsequent meeting of the council's zoo licensing panel, members were told that a licence must be refused if the zoo was a threat to health or safety among nearby residents, or to law and order. The sheriff, Cllr Edna Adams stated plainly that she did not like zoos and did not like to see animals in captivity. A bear could run amok and kill people. Councillors nevertheless renewed the zoo operating licence from 31 December 1980, for a further five years, on hearing that one or more of the larger animals would be phased out. The pumas had been up for sale for two years but their owners had been unable to find suitable homes for them and were reluctant to have them destroyed. Large monkeys would be replaced by smaller ones. Rent would be £5,500 annually for the first three years and then be reviewed. New admission charges were also agreed.

In 1983 the Pettits left the zoo after a decade and the licence was transferred to Mr David Flower who had already been its manager for two years. A keen bird fancier, he was writing a book about parrots.

Opposition gained momentum. In September of that year the RSPCA's chief wildlife officer called the zoo; '... a horrendous seaside menagerie whose days were numbered'. Speaking at an Animal Aid meeting he said the zoo should be forced to close unless a lot of money was spent improving cages and compounds. It displayed animals in the same way a greengrocer displayed oranges and apples. The site was all wrong in the first place. Keeping a zoo was a very expensive business, and any owner unable to cope should not do so. Activists conducted leaflet and poster campaigns and daubed slogans on the zoo walls. On one regrettable occasion, it was alleged, they threw paint stripper over two zoo vehicles.

The zoo suffered too from the theft of valuable birds (see Crime and Law Enforcement) and, in the autumn of 1984, David Flower lost his best breeding wallaby in a freak accident. It was struck in the chest by a missile – possibly lobbed by children trying to dislodge conkers from chestnut trees adjacent to its open-topped cage – and the unlucky creature died from the resulting haemorrhage.

One Saturday afternoon in 1985 David Flower closed the premises rather than face an angry demonstration by teenage girls, admitting he shared their concern for the larger animals whose numbers he had been trying to reduce for the last two years. He had disposed of the bears, but it was very difficult to find new homes for some others and it could not be done overnight.

When the zoo was due to be considered for a new-style four-year operational licence in September 1985, the owners reiterated that the criticism of Poole Zoo was not borne out by the facts. A new partner, George Edmonds, had a persuasive twenty-five-year pedigree, having in turn held posts as assistant director at Blackpool Zoo, head warden at Windsor Safari Park and a supervisor at Chessington Zoo. He had also been an official RSPCA inspector and held a Department of the Environment licence as a zoo inspector. He had to admit, however, that the facilities were too small for the larger animals and said that he hoped to move his one and only penguin to a new home at Merley Bird Gardens, and to find other zoos or parks to take the leopards within six months.

The zoo's adversaries remained implacable. A total of 416 signed three petitions or sent individual letters. Bill Bean and his wife Olive, representing Poole anti-zoo ratepayers, described the zoo as: 'A tacky place made of chicken wire, breeze-block and corrugated plastic where the animals – some in solitary confinement – can't even see the sky and many don't even have grass underfoot'.

They urged the five-member panel of Poole councillors to close the zoo at once. Letters from residents living close by reiterated the complaint of danger from escaping animals (and disease), also referring to, 'terrible, prison-like and disgraceful conditions, the despair of animals and small enclosures'. A local spokesman for Animal Aid, said that the zoo's offer to get rid of its leopards as soon as a home could be found for them did not alter conditions at the zoo for the smaller animals which remained, nor would it help to meet their psychological needs.

More than 500 supporters, including 200 season ticket holders, commended the zoo's educational and amenity value, saying it was well run and not a nuisance. Still a Zoo Check report branded the zoo's owners as 'misguided amateurs', but this was rebutted furiously and the critics referred to the zoo's success at breeding Asian short-clawed otters, Lanner falcons and Florida bobcats (the only ones known to have bred successfully in captivity in the UK).

So the dispute continued. In 1990 there were renewed calls for the zoo's closure. Responding to a couple of surveys carried out by the University of Surrey for Poole Council, in which people were asked to list their likes and dislikes, the zoo was again described as 'tacky'. A former RSPCA chief wildlife officer, Stefan Ormrod, speaking for the anti-captivity campaigners Zoo Check, claimed the zoo was 'a frightening fire hazard' and warned that during opening hours 'the public would be seriously at risk'. Animal Aid spokesman Malcolm Venn said that wild animals belonged in the wild and not in 'a sawn-off shanty called Poole Park Zoo'.

In 1992 the Federation of Zoological Gardens, which represented fifty-three zoos, expressed its concerns about Poole Park Zoo; but then, in a confidential letter to Poole's tourism sub-committee on Tuesday 28 July, the federation observed that only assessments by inspectors under the Zoo Licensing Act were valid, and questioned the validity and bias of the opinion of Zoo Check. Councillors, whether personally for or against zoos, strove to sort objective facts from anecdotal prejudice, hyperbole, fulmination, rave and rant.

In April 1993 it looked as if the zoo would finally close after Fernthrush Ltd, whose licence still had years to run, hit money problems and ceased trading, but the council's officers granted a fresh licence to the newly formed Poole Zoological Park Ltd. As the public had been excluded from the meeting granting this licence, some critics alleged the decision had been made in secret, but the acting amenities officer explained that open licence hearings were unworkable (as visitors had continually to leave the room before debate of each and every confidential licensing condition).

By now even some councillors felt there was no remaining justification for keeping the zoo open. After thirty-one years, the last ten or more of which had been unedifying, the zoo closed in February 1994 when the leaseholder failed to pay his rent. The cages and compounds were cleared out virtually overnight. Animal Rights' campaigners celebrated the zoo's disappearance, while many regular visitors lamented its loss. All the animals were ultimately found new homes and none had to be put down. Despite lingering notions to bring small animals back to the park in some sort of pets corner for children, or as an owl sanctuary, councillors ultimately agreed to demolish the existing buildings and never again to use the site as a zoo or bird park.

A trial reed bed filters run-off water from the railway embankment and footpath into the saltwater boating lake. (Geoffrey Budworth)

The saltwater lake creates species-specific conditions for a variety of birds. (Geoffrey Budworth)

AFTERWORD

We are tomorrow's past.
Mary Webb, English novelist, 1881–1927

In 1995, after many years of lobbying by locals, Poole Park was designated a Conservation Area, and in 2002 also a Grade II English Heritage Listed park and garden, its Victorian layout and features deemed to be of national importance. Although there are no listed buildings within the park, Seldown Lodge, East Gate Lodge and the cricket pavilion, as well as all the ornamental gates themselves, became 'local listed buildings'.

Matching the pursuit of excellence that inspired Poole Corporation to create Poole Park in the first place, the council has submitted an application to achieve Green Flag status for the park. This is similar to the Blue Flag accreditation scheme applicable to seaside beaches, and is increasingly seen as a benchmark for high quality.

Linking the harbour-side recreational areas of Baiter and Whitecliff with Poole Park by signage, footpaths and trails, despite their physical separation by the railway embankment, is another work in progress.

The park is a designated flood plain. If the forecast climate change aggravated by the actions of humankind were to create a catastrophic rise in sea levels, then it is likely that Parkstone Bay would expand to inundate the amenity, reclaiming it for Poole harbour once more. Meanwhile, it remains one of the South of England's finest public parks. In June 2006, I overheard a motorist seated in his stationary car, chatting on a mobile phone, say, 'Yes, well, I'm currently parked in Poole Park, under a shady tree, collecting myself.' Long may we all be able to do so.

> I wish I had the voice of Horace★
> To sing of Tom and Dick and Doris
> (Ancestral folk, real names forgot)
> Who bequeathed us Poole Park, lakes, the lot.
>
> I'd also praise, extol, applaud
> Those who today across the board
> In diverse ways still plan and plot
> To cultivate Poole Park, lakes, the lot.
>
> And when I'm dead and underground,
> I trust some scribblers then around
> Will in their turn rejoice they got
> Our legacy – Poole Park, lakes, the lot.

★ Horace: Roman lyric poet and satirist whose work is distinguished by its style, wit and good sense.

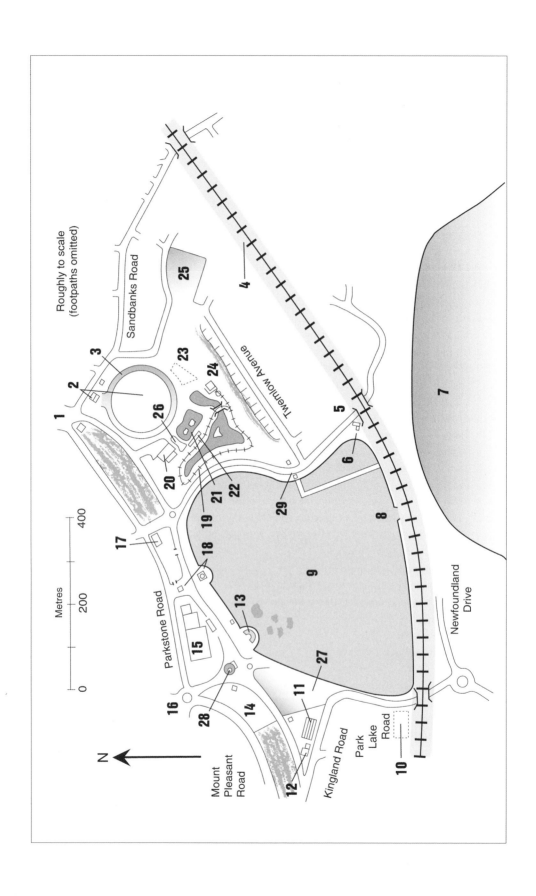

Roughly to scale
(footpaths omitted)

Sandbanks Road

Wemlow Avenue

Parkstone Road

Mount
Pleasant
Road

Kingland Road

Park
Lake
Road

Newfoundland
Drive

Metres

0   200   400

N

POOLE PARK GUIDED WALK

Walking is the favourite sport of the good and the wise.

A.L. Rowse, English historian, 1903–1997

KEY TO MAP

1	East Gate and lodge
2	Cricket pavilion and pitch
3	Cycle track
4	London (Waterloo) to Poole and Weymouth railway and embankment
5	The keyhole bridge
6	Model yacht lagoon and club HQ
7	Parkstone Bay
8	Sluice channel (or 'bunny')
9	Saltwater boating lake
10	Site of defunct open-air swimming pool
11	Chestnut Nursery
12	Seldown Gate and lodge
13	Mezza Luna Restaurant
14	Putting green
15	Bowling greens and pavilion and tennis courts
16	Norton's Gate, leading down to the French-style fountain
17	Albert cottages
18	Mounbatten and war memorials
19	Freshwater lake
20	Cygnet (originally Swan Lake) Café
21	Duck pond
22	Miniature railway station
23	Site of defunct zoo
24	Engine shed and turntable, leading to miniature train track
25	Copse Close playing field
26	Cygnet children's play area
27	West field children's play area
28	The fountain
29	Whitecliff Gate

Access to the Park by Car:

The park has five gateways, three of which are accessible to road traffic, namely: the East Gate (in only), the Seldown Gate (two-way) and the Whitecliff Road Gate (also two-way) via the keyhole bridge beneath the railway embankment. These vehicular access points are closed to traffic during weekday mornings (6–10 a.m.) to stop the park being used as a short cut and to discourage parking by town-centre workers.

There are short/medium-stay car-parking areas within the park, as well as alongside certain designated sections of roadway, also behind the Central Park Café (still called the Swan Lake or Cygnet Café by some who recall its previous names) and beside the Mezza Luna Restaurant.

By Land Train:

This starts and ends its round trip at Poole Quay, entering and leaving the park by the Seldown Gate. On its outward leg it stops at the putting and crazy golf courses. the boating lake, and the Cygnet Café car park, before retracing its route (leaving the park to take a tour of the town). Drivers may prefer to leave their vehicles in car parks outside the park; and, on occasions when the park hosts a major event and is closed to all traffic, the land train is the only way to ride.

By Bus:

Poole's town centre 'Route One' blue hopper buses run every fifteen minutes on a circular route, linking bus and rail stations, car parks, shopping areas and the park. Bargain fares or an all-day (hop-on, hop-off) ticket make it a cheap and convenient option.

On Foot:

As well as the major entrances there are at least another nine less impressive, but nevertheless handy, gateways into the park for pedestrians. There is also a subway leading to and from the Baiter harbour-side area, and a footpath from the Express Holiday Inn via the new eco-village development.

Distance of the guided walk:	about 2km (1¼ miles)
Duration:	one hour

Beginning at the Central Park Café, your route goes clockwise to include all aspects of the park – ornamental gateways, historic buildings, freshwater and boating lakes, wildlife, and activities (boating and bowling, model yachts, the miniature railway, putting and tennis).

Start by the two red telephone boxes (see also Sundries in the Glossary). Find your way to the open-air patio of tables and chairs in front of the Central Park Café and walk towards the miniature railway track. Look right to locate a pair of old-fashioned red telephone kiosks. Either cross the grass directly to them (mind the goose droppings) or follow the footpath.

These are the K6 'Jubilee' model telephone boxes which were once a familiar sight on British streets. Designed by leading architect Sir Giles Gilbert (1880–1960), who won a Post Office competition to do so, they commemorate the Silver Jubilee of King George V in 1935. There are four within the park.

> *Turn right and follow the road.*

AVENUE OF HORSE CHESTNUT TREES (see also Trees, Shrubs and Plants)

This section of road was once lined with an avenue of horse chestnut trees but many have now been felled due to their age and condition.

> *Walk along the footway beside the road as it curves left, past a small rock garden and waterfall, to the East Gate.*

EAST GATE LODGE (see Entrances, Gates and Lodges)

The East Gate entrance which has a small bungalow, built in 1888 to be occupied by one or other of the ground staff, conceals a relic of the park's opening.

> *Go out of the gate, turn sharp left and peer through the railings.*

On the north wall of the lodge see an ornamental stone memorial in the form of a long scroll which describes how the park was donated to the town.

Before re-entering the park, pause to admire the gateway with its handsome brick and stone pillars, inset with weathered sea-life panels, and topped with eagles and ornamental lamps. These terracotta ornamentations were created by George Jennings, a potter based at Hamworthy (or South Western Pottery, Parkstone) who had previously been employed as chief sanitary engineer for the Great Exhibition in 1951.

Between the two world wars a woman sat on the footway here, selling home-made sweets and postcards to Poole and district to passers-by.

(The imposing building across the road from you was opened in 1931 and contains the Borough of Poole's civic offices, committee rooms and meeting chambers, from which Poole Park is managed.)

> *Re-enter the park, and bear left to walk clockwise around the perimeter of the cricket ground.*

THE FIELD GUN (see Sundries)

Across the road from the East Lodge, parked on the grass, there was once a German 125mm breech-loading field gun that had been given to Poole as a trophy from the First World War. The gun remained in the park until 1928.

CRICKET PITCH AND PAVILION (see Sport and Recreation)

From 1902 county matches were played here, until the lack of maintenance imposed by the Second World War resulted in the drainage silting up. Later it was restored for county fixtures to resume from time to time. The clock on the cricket pavilion was added in 1960. The tiled brick building beyond the pavilion is a pumping station for the Wessex Water Co.

CYCLE TRACK (see Sport and Recreation)

The broad pathway on which you are walking is a more or less circular cycle track 534m (a little less than one third of a mile) in circumference. It is one of only a few such tracks to survive, having been constructed in 1888/89, and a reminder of the fashionable trend for bicycling – both recreational and competitive – that burgeoned with the Victorians.

COPSE CLOSE FIELD

Hit a six from this section of the cycle track and the ball could land in the playing field beside the residential cul de sac called Copse Close. After the path goes right, look to your left and glimpse this adjunct to the main body of Poole Park, surrounded by mature trees and shrubs, which was added in 1930.

(The grassy space between the Copse Close playing field and some fencing ahead is the site of the park's defunct zoo.)

> *Continue bearing right, following the cycle track around, until you meet with a small children's play area.*

CYGNET PLAY AREA (see Children's Play Areas)

This facility for younger children was created by the Friends of Poole Park in November 2005.

On your immediate left is the duck pond with its two islands, which was once fenced to protect its more exotic wildlife, such as black swans and muscovy ducks, from predation by foxes.

Pause to look at the miniature railway station, completed for Easter 1962, and maybe buy a postcard or a bag of bird food there, or take a ride on the train. The job of building this replacement of the original 1949 station was given to the brick-laying tutor at Poole Technical College and the woodwork was undertaken by Poole Joinery.

THE MINIATURE RAILWAY (see Miniature Railway)

The railway began operating on Saturday 9 April 1949 (but not, at first, on Sundays). The cost of a ticket for an adult to ride was 1s. and for a child 6d. These fares remained the same for twenty years. Daily steam operation ceased at the end of the 1965 season and diesel had wholly replaced it by 1969.

> *Go left, following the railway, with the duck pond on your left and the railway track on your right.*

FRESHWATER LAKE (see Freshwater Lake)

The larger expanse of water on your right, originally fed by one or two existing springs, was dug out to create the present freshwater lake totalling 2 acres with a leg-of-mutton shape.

> *Cross the railway bridge over the narrow neck that separates the smaller portion of the freshwater lake on your left from the much larger area (with an island) on your right.*

RAILWAY BRIDGE (see Miniature Railway)

This concrete bridge carrying the miniature railway track across the freshwater lake's narrow neck was installed soon after the end of the Second World War. It replaced an earlier rustic version destroyed in the mid-1940s by a bomb dropped from a German raider.

> *Follow the railway track as it bends right (leaving behind you the engine shed and tiny turntable). If you come face-to-face with a train loaded with passengers, wave to the younger riders.*

Here are numerous places to stand or sit and watch the water birds.

> *Shortly after the line intersects the path from left to right, cross the road and go left, walking beside the saltwater lake.*

See the raised and curved reed bed that was created in 2007 with sediment dredged from the lake bed held in place by willow hurdles. This is one of two such reed beds where water polluted with oil and rubber from roads as well as other undesirable debris, discharges, via drains and surface run-off, into the lake. The reed beds with their vegetation have been located so as to act as filters and so combat any reduction in water quality of the lake as a whole.

> *Leave the park temporarily by the Whitecliff Gate.*

THE WHITECLIFF GATE (see Entrances, Gates and Lodges)

Located close by the curiously named Twemlow Avenue, it matches in style the East Gate you have already visited and the Seldown and Norton's Gates which you have yet to see.

> *Continue beside the saltwater lake towards the railway bridge that crosses the road with a narrow arch.*

THE KEYHOLE BRIDGE (see Entrances, Gates and Lodges)

During its pre-1890 negotiations, the council asked the railway company to construct this access to and from the park, large enough for the passage of a carriage (even if it did have its base below sea level). The maximum height clearance is 7ft 6in (roughly 2.3m). This awkward vehicular pinch point reduces vehicles to a single alternate line, on a first-come, first-served basis.

CAUTION – When approaching the keyhole bridge, it would be prudent to put dogs on leads. This is not only to prevent them from investigating any radio-controlled yachts, but also because the sluice-gate channel further along the footpath can lure dogs into it, when they find it difficult to climb out again without human help.

> *Turn right onto the footpath in front of the Model Yacht Club.*

POOLE RADIO YACHT CLUB (see Model Yacht Club)

There has been a model yacht and boat club here, adjacent to the keyhole bridge since perhaps 1900 although the current single-storey, L-shaped wooden structure within its wire-mesh compound, sporting its circular burgee sign, dates from 1950. See the white-sailed wind van atop the white flag pole. The rectangular catwalk that isolates this corner of the saltwater lake was built by the local authority to replace an earlier wooden one carried away by gales in 1923.

Radio controlled (RC) yachting was truly launched when small and light transistors replaced the clumsy and less reliable thermionic valves and 27Mhz 'digital' equipment became readily available in the 1960s.

> *Follow the footpath with the railway embankment on your left, and the lake on your right.*

THE FOOTPATH (see Saltwater Lake)

The trains that come and go on the mainline railway embankment are travelling between London (Waterloo) and Weymouth.

> *Halfway along the footpath pause to examine the sluices.*

THE SLUICES (see Saltwater Lake)

Opening these sluice gates makes it possible to flush the boating lake periodically and so freshen it by allowing the tides to achieve a partial empty-and-fill sequence. This minimises the swarms of midges that otherwise might breed here. Similarly the depth can be reduced for maintenance work around the perimeter of the lake by opening the gates and simply waiting for low tide to expose the surrounding foreshore.

> *On reaching Park Lake Road, go right, but note the pedestrian subway going beneath the railway embankment to the Baitor.*

PARK LAKE ROAD (see Saltwater Lake)

At this corner of the saltwater lake is a derelict site that, despite the development of the nearby eco-village, has not been built upon because it is part of the park. This was the site of an outdoor swimming pool from around 1930 until 1961, and will be used from 2008 by the junior section of Poole Harbour Canoe Club.

The owners and occupiers of the row of large post-First World War houses on the landward side of this road no doubt relish the fact that their extraordinary view is unlikely ever to be altered or obstructed.

> *On reaching the gateway leading to a children's play area, turn left up the slight gradient of Kingland Road on the right-hand footway.*

CHESTNUT NURSERY (see Trees, Shrubs and Plants)

Pause by the entrance to this site with its mature Leylandii hedge (*Cupressocyparis Leylandii*). Prior to 1998 it was occupied by the Poole Park Nursery growing plants for use within the borough and the park. When the contract was lost in the new ethos of compulsory competitive tendering, the 2.2-acre site grew derelict with disuse over two to three years.

In October 2001 it was taken over by the Chestnut Nursery, one of two such locations (the other being the Cherry Tree Nursery in Bournemouth) operated by the Sheltered Work Opportunities Project. With its five greenhouses repaired and restored and the site cleared, it sells a variety of perennials, shrubs, ornamental grasses and seasonal crops. Plant sales alone cannot cover its expenses and so the nursery's volunteers are committed to time-consuming fundraising and donations to continue their valuable work. You might like to go in and buy something.

> *Re-enter the park through the Seldown Gate.*

SELDOWN GATE (see Entrances, Lakes and Lodges)

Built in 1888, together with the East Gate Lodge, this larger building was occupied by the first gatekeeper Albert Saville until his death in 1907. It has a cart house and stable block.

Notice on the side of the house the round, stone coat of arms featuring a mermaid (minus arms) atop a medieval helm, beneath which is a shield with three sea shells and a dolphin. Under those is a scroll with the Latin motto *Ad Morem Villae de Poole* (According to the Custom of the Town of Poole).

At the front of this building, with its red bricks and stone quoins, is a shield bearing the date AD 1888 on the left-hand gable, and a tablet affixed to the wall on the left of the front door commemorating the park's opening in 1890.

> *Walk downhill, with the opportunity for a toilet break on the right-hand side after approximately 200m.*

The grassy West Field area on your right, with its children's play area, has been the site of many events and was where the grandstand was located for Poole's 1952 pageant.

> *Pass another Gilbert Scott red telephone box and the first of the park's several 'sleeping policemen'.*

'SLEEPING POLICEMEN' (see Traffic)
In 1994 these new double-hump speed restrictions were introduced to the park's roads and vehicular suspension systems, combined with pinch points that enforced a single alternate flow of traffic. They are as high as the footway kerbs so that, not only do they reduce car speeds, but they provide a raised level for pedestrians (especially those who are less mobile) to cross without the need for pedestrian-crossing signs and markings.

PUTTING GREEN AND CRAZY GOLF (see Sport and Recreation, and Wartime)
The putting green on the left-hand side was created in 1929 and the crazy golf much later.

In May 1944 a large fuel-storage tank was built near to the putting green to refuel the US Navy's sixty coastguard cutters waiting to take part in the D-Day Normandy landings.

> *As a fresh view of the saltwater lake opens up, see the cluster of five islets.*

In 2007 the lake bed was partially dredged and, the spoil used to create these islets, plus two raised reed beds (one of which you saw earlier). These are contained within willow hurdles that will eventually biodegrade, by which time they should be stabilised by the root systems of vegetation. This planting began in May 2007 and will continue for two or three years. Sea aster, sea rush, sea clubrush and common reed were chosen as best suited to the constantly changing salinity of the lake. These islets will, it is hoped, become wildlife habitat and safe nesting sites for a variety of birds.

MEZZA LUNA RESTAURANT (see Catering)
A glass-fronted waterside restaurant overlooking the lake opened in 2007. It is owned and operated by Adrian Forte, whose family have been catering in the park for sixty years, and represents a £2 million investment in the restaurant beside the lake together with the revamped Central Park Café and indoor ice rink where your walk began. See the two mature holm oak (*Quercus ilex*) trees that the crescent-shaped Mezza Luna Restaurant (Italian for half or crescent moon) was designed to preserve.

> *Divert and go left in front of the fountain, up a gentle slope, ascending the stone steps, to view Norton's Gate from the outside.*

NORTON'S GATE (see Entrances, Gates and Lodges)

In the late 1960s the imposing gate pillars that had previously adorned this entrance were taken down as part of an improved road and roundabout scheme, leaving only pedestrian access. The avenue of trees between the bowling and putting greens remained an important landscape feature of the park (but minus the bandstand built near the water in 1889). The gateway was restored in 1990 as part of the park's centenary celebrations. Workers digging there recovered pieces of terracotta from four of the pillars, and these were used to restore the Whitecliff Road entrance.

Norton's Gate was named in memory of Victorian philanthropist John James Norton, a self-made timber magnate.

> *Re-enter the park and walk back down to the fountain.*

THE FOUNTAIN (see Fountain)

This French-style fountain was a gift to the town from Lord Wimborne (grandson of the first holder of that title) and was unveiled by him on 8 June 1990. Lord Wimborne and his second wife donated £30,000 to buy the structure but it then cost the borough an estimated £60,000 to install it.

> *Bear left, with the Mezza Luna Restaurant on you right and the bowls club on your left.*

BOWLING GREEN (see Sport and Recreation)

The two bowling greens of Cumberland turf were opened here in 1930 and within a few years Poole Park Bowling Club achieved national fame by winning the Pairs' Championships of the English Bowling Association twice in successive years and Mr E.P. Baker became the singles champion of England in 1932, 1946, 1952 and 1955. The club's greens were also good enough for the final rounds of the National Triples' Championship in 1958 and 1959. The stylish pavilion cost £240,000 and was opened on Friday 22 June 2001.

BOATING (see Boating)

Generations of visitors to the park have hired canoes, kayaks, rowing or sailing dinghies, and gone afloat from the waterside here. Boating activity lapsed, however, for several years and only returned in 2007. Then Rockley Watersports, the premier sailing school in the south of England (located in Poole harbour) won the contract to operate within the park, where its highly qualified and experienced instructors provide a range of equipment hire, taster sessions, short courses and evening sessions, for everyone from 'pay-and-play' park visitors to organised school parties.

> *Cross the road opposite the boating area to the information kiosk.*

KIOSK (see Sundries)

This Art Deco style structure was built during the Second World War as an ice-cream kiosk. It was renovated and restored to active use by the Friends of Poole Park, backed by Poole Borough Council members and officers, and reopened on Wednesday 23 January 2008.

THE 'FALLING DOWN' TREE (see Children's Play)

This horizontal Corsican or black pine (*Pinus nigra 'maritima'*) has provided play and climbing opportunities for generations of children. It is one of the memorable features of the park and features in the Friends of Poole Park logo.

TENNIS (see Sport and Recreation, Fashion and Wartime)

Before permanent courts were created, summer tennis was originally played with nets erected on the grass area across the road from the bowling greens. In winter the tennis nets might be replaced by hockey or lacrosse pitches. During the Second World War the tennis courts were dug up and used by gardeners for vegetable allotments, and it was sometime after the end of hostilities before they were relaid.

> *Pass yet another Gilbert Scott red telephone box across the road from the tennis courts. Turn right to pay your respects at the two war memorials.*

THE WAR MEMORIAL (see War Memorials)

This was unveiled at 3 p.m. on Sunday 16 October 1927 and, minus individual names, serves as a timeless symbol for to all from the town who suffered and died on land and sea, or in the air, for freedom and in defence of their country in any conflict.

> *Cross the road to view the Mountbatten Memorial.*

THE MOUNTBATTEN MEMORIAL (see War Memorials)

Unveiled by Lady Pamela Hicks (daughter of Lord Louis Mountbatten) in a dedication ceremony in 1980, this later memorial recalls those of the so-called 'Forgotten Army' who fell in battle or who have suffered since from physical or mental injuries. It also commemorates Lord Mountbatten, who as Supreme Allied Commander, SE Asia, led them through three years of jungle warfare in the Burma campaign of the Second World War. He was patron of the Burma Star Association from its foundation in the 1950s until he was deliberately targeted and killed by an IRA bomb in 1979. The Kohima Epitaph (words attributed to John Maxwell Edwards, 1875–1958) inscribed upon the plinth is associated with Burma Star memorials around the world.

(If you walk the extra distance to exit the park for a few minutes and stand looking back down towards original war memorial and its backdrop of the saltwater lake, you can see the dedicated Memorial Gates.)

> *Continue along the road, back towards the Cygnet Café.*

(At the north-east corner of the saltwater lake, see the second raised reed bed. On your left is access to a concealed rose garden.)

At the mini-roundabout, angle right on the footpath that crosses the miniature railway track to reach the corner of the freshwater lake.

THE 'GOOSE LADY' PLAQUE (see Wildlife)

Anna Beiner from Wimbourne frequented the water's edge and fed the birds for many years. When she died, aged ninety-four, she left what little funds she had to continue feeding them, and in recognition of her selflessness a close friend, Ria Sanders, approached local companies and residents to fund a tribute to her. The Borough of Poole, local stonemason Anthony Ives and the Bournemouth Engraving and Trophy Centre all had a hand in producing this plaque.

> *Your walk ends here.*

Approaching the war memorial gardens. (Geoffrey Budworth)

THE FRIENDS OF POOLE PARK

The Friends of Poole Park is a voluntary organisation formed early in 2002 by individuals with a special interest in the development and future of the park. Their objectives are to:

- Encourage public awareness, use and enjoyment of the park
- Foster and assist the park's development, raising funds and acquiring assets for the purpose
- Promote the park as a tourist attraction for visitors and holiday-makers to Poole and the surrounding area
- Support and aid the Borough of Poole in its management of the park

The Friends believe theirs is a worthwhile endeavour that will have a major impact on both the local community and park users alike. They keep in touch and informed by means of a regular newsletter, periodic meetings and social events. New members are always welcome and the annual membership fee is modest (although donations are also gladly received).

ACKNOWLEDGEMENTS

This look at Poole Park is a concentrated essence, distilled and flavoured from a considerably greater collection of material from a variety of sources. In the process I pestered and inconvenienced numerous individuals whom I now thank publicly for their time, patience, knowledge, advice and guidance (freely given): Maria Burns, artist and illustrator; Chris Bullen and Brian Merrifield, miniature train owners and operators; Adrian Forte, catering supremo; Scott Harrison, Michaela Horsfield and Ed Perkins, all from Bournemouth's *Daily Echo and Advertiser*; Clare Freeman, Mike Gotobed, Keith Guy, Richard Hein, Paul Hillman, John Marter, Richard Nicholson, all from Borough of Poole; Bob Lister, chairman of Friends of Poole Park; Iris Morris, local historian and author; Pat Parker, Waterfront Museum; Roger Sansom, Friends of Poole Park Miniature Railway; Dave Shutler, grandson of Arthur Vincent Shutler; Geoff Tapper, boat-hire owner and operator; John Trew and Derek White, Poole Radio Yacht Club.

PICTURE CREDITS

The more than ninety illustrations appearing in this book were brought together from several sources. Of these, the following all quoted me a generous reduction in their usual copyright payments for use of their pictures: Michael J. Allen Photography; the *Bournemouth Daily Echo* (Newsprints Ltd); Andrew Hawkes (collector, historian and author); and Salisbury Photo Imaging Ltd.

I am also indebted to the following who generously supplied images free of charge: Danny Byrne, Dorset-based Artist and Illustrator; Brian Merrifiel; Poole Radio Yacht Club (Commodore: Derek White); Geoff Tapper.

All of the remaining illustrations are either my own snapshots, or from my private collection of old postcards, none of which has any details of either publisher or printer whose permission might otherwise have been sought for their inclusion here.

If I have omitted to mention anyone – abject apologies. You know who you are, so contact me. I owe you a signed complimentary copy of this book.

SOURCES & FURTHER READING

BOOKS

Bear, Magdalen, *Days, Months and Years – a Perpetual Calendar for the Past, Present and Future*, Tarquin Publications, 1989

Burgess, Michael J., *Behind the Wheel – A Romance of the Motor Car*, Michael O'Mara Books Ltd, 2000

Carter, H.S., *I Call to Mind*, J. Looker Ltd, Poole, 1949

Ewing, Elizabeth, *History of 20th Century Fashion*, first published 1974, B.T. Batsford Ltd with a revised 3rd edition (1992) by Alice Mackrell

Guy, Keith, *Poole Park Railways, the First Fifty Years, 1949–1999*, Friends of Poole Park Railway, 1999

Hansard, Peter and Silver, Burton, *What Bird did That?*, Grub Street, London, 1991

Hawkes, Andrew, *Memories of Old Poole*, A.D. Hawkes, 1979

Hiller, John, *A Portfolio of Old Poole*, Poole Historical Trust, 1983

Peacock, John, *Men's Fashions – the Complete Source Book*, Thames and Hudson, 1996

Rose, Clare, *Children's Clothes*, B.T. Batsford Ltd, 1989

MAGAZINES & ARTICLES

Bournemouth Echo, Poole Park (1890–1990) Centenary Festival (2nd–10th June) a programme in the newspaper archives, 2000–2006

Department of Amenities & Recreation *Poole Park, the People's Park* a draft consultative document, 1989

Dwyer, Jack, 'Doing a Ton through Poole Park, Part II' in *Motoring Magazine*, April 1990

Footpaths lead to peacefully sequestered places. (Geoffrey Budworth)

Other titles published by The History Press

Haunted Poole
JULIE HARWOOD

From heart-stopping accounts of apparitions, manifestations and related supernatural phenomena to first-hand encounters with ghouls and spirits, this collection of stories contains new and well-known spooky tales from in and around Poole, including the town's own tragic Romeo and Juliet tale, legendary Poole pirate Harry Paye and his ghostly galleon, and ghoulish beggars that wander the streets.

978 07524 4503 8

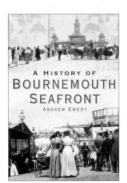

A History of Bournemouth Seafront
ANDREW EMERY

For nearly 200 years Bournemouth's award-winning seafront has embraced generations of visitors, developing an unrivalled reputation for outstanding natural beauty, glorious golden sands and simple seaside pleasures. This story traces the coastline from its very beginnings as a remote and barren heathland through early development into a health and spa resort to its rise as Britain's favourite family beach.

978 07524 4717 9

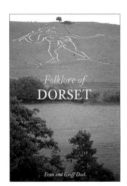

Folklore of Dorset
FRAN AND GEOFF DOEL

Folklore of Dorset explores the rich heritage of the county's traditions, seasonal customs and songs. Included are saints' lore and smugglers, wife sales, wrecking, witchcraft, wise men and West Gallery Music, hill figures, hempseed divination and holy wells, mummers plays, May garlands and maypoles, Oosers and Oak Apple Day, bonfires and Beating the Bounds.

978 07524 3989 1

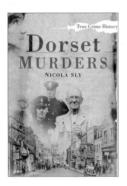

Dorset Murders
NICOLA SLY

Life in the largely rural county of Dorset has not always been idyllic, for over the years it has experienced numerous murders, some of which are little known outside the county borders, others that have shocked the nation. Illustrated with fifty illustrations, *Dorset Murders* examines some of these historic cases and is sure to appeal to anyone interested in the shady side of county's history.

978 07509 5107 4

If you are interested in purchasing these or other books published by The History Press you can place orders directly through our website:

www.thehistorypress.co.uk